CAMPAIGN • 225

MESSINES 1917

The zenith of siege warfare

ALEXANDER TURNER

ILLUSTRATED BY PETER DENNIS

Series editor Marcus Cowper

First published in Great Britain in 2010 by Osprey Publishing,
Midland House, West Way, Botley, Oxford OX2 0PH, UK
44-02 23rd St, Suite 219, Long Island City, NY 11101, USA
E-mail: info@ospreypublishing.com

A CIP catalogue record for this book is available from the British Library.

ISBN: 978 1 84603 845 7

PDF e-book ISBN: 978 1 84908 290 7

Editorial by Ilios Publishing Ltd, Oxford, UK (www.iliospublishing.com)
Page layout by The Black Spot
Index by Margaret Vaudrey
Typeset in Sabon and Myriad Pro
Maps by Bounford.com
3D bird's-eye views by The Black Spot
Battlescene illustrations by Peter Dennis
Originated by PDQ Media
Printed in China through Worldprint

10 11 12 13 14   10 9 8 7 6 5 4 3 2 1

THE WOODLAND TRUST

Osprey Publishing are supporting the Woodland Trust, the UK's leading
woodland conservation charity, by funding the dedication of trees.

DEDICATION

For my mother Josephine.

ACKNOWLEDGEMENTS

I am grateful to all the historians who have put so much research into Great
War tunnelling, which otherwise would have been impenetrable with the
time and resources I had available. Once again, the advice and assistance of
Phillip Robinson was of inestimable value and my thanks go to Jack Sheldon
for permission to use his translations – they bring the German experience to
English eyes. Staff at the Imperial War Museum and National Archives were
exemplary as ever, as was Rebecca Nash at the Royal Engineer Museum. Ian
Passingham and Ronald Pawly were also of assistance in my research. Henry
Elstub and Will Mace were excellent company in Ypres; we nearly got through
the wine list. Thanks as always to Crispin Daly for his German language skills,
Peter Dennis for being so engaging and Marcus Cowper, now a firm friend.

AUTHOR'S NOTE

In describing military formations the text of this narrative conforms to the
convention of using capital letters only in the formal titles of units. Generic
references to corps, divisions, brigades and regiments etc. remain in the
lower case as demonstrated here. Regional affiliations with British divisions
will be specified only the first time that formation is mentioned. Unless part
of the author's collection, all photographs are reproduced with the kind
permission of the Imperial War Museum or Royal Engineers Museum.
Readers may be interested to know that many of the IWM 'E' series
(official Australian) photographs in this book were taken by Frank Hurley –
photographer to Sir Ernest Shackleton's famous 1914 Antarctic expedition.

IMPERIAL WAR MUSEUM COLLECTIONS

Many of the photos in this book come from the Imperial War Museum's
huge collections which cover all aspects of conflict involving Britain
and the Commonwealth since the start of the twentieth century.
These rich resources are available online to search, browse and buy
at www.iwmcollections.org.uk. In addition to Collections Online,
you can visit the Visitor Rooms where you can explore over 8 million
photographs, thousands of hours of moving images, the largest sound
archive of its kind in the world, thousands of diaries and letters written by
people in wartime, and a huge reference library. To make an appointment,
call (020) 7416 5320, or e-mail mail@iwm.org.uk.
Imperial War Museum www.iwm.org.uk

ARTIST'S NOTE

Readers may care to note that the original paintings from which the
colour plates in this book were prepared are available for private sale.
The Publishers retain all reproduction copyright whatsoever.
All enquiries should be addressed to:

Peter Dennis, Fieldhead, The Park, Mansfield, Notts, NG18 2AT, UK

The Publishers regret that they can enter into no correspondence upon
this matter.

Key to military symbols

×××××	××××	×××	××	×	III	II
Army Group	Army	Corps	Division	Brigade	Regiment	Battalion
I	•••	••	•	⊠	•	◧
Company/Battery	Platoon	Section	Squad	Infantry	Artillery	Cavalry
Airborne	Unit HQ	Air defence	Air Force	Air mobile	Air transportable	Amphibious
Anti-tank	Armour	Air aviation	Bridging	Engineer	Headquarters	Maintenance
Medical	Missile	Mountain	Navy	Nuclear, biological, chemical	Ordnance	Parachute
Reconnaissance	Signal	Supply	Transport movement	Rocket artillery	Air defence artillery	

Key to unit identification

Unit identifier | ⊠ | Parent unit
Commander
(+) with added elements
(−) less elements

FOR A CATALOGUE OF ALL BOOKS PUBLISHED BY OSPREY MILITARY
AND AVIATION PLEASE CONTACT:

NORTH AMERICA
Osprey Direct, c/o Random House Distribution Center, 400 Hahn
Road, Westminster, MD 21157
E-mail: uscustomerservice@ospreypublishing.com

ALL OTHER REGIONS
Osprey Direct, The Book Service Ltd, Distribution Centre, Colchester
Road, Frating Green, Colchester, Essex, CO7 7DW
E-mail: customerservice@ospreypublishing.com

www.ospreypublishing.com

CONTENTS

ORIGINS OF THE CAMPAIGN   5

CHRONOLOGY   12

OPPOSING COMMANDERS   15
Playing the hand that's dealt . The British . The Germans

OPPOSING FORCES   19
The Germans . Mine warfare . The British . Orders of battle

OPPOSING PLANS   36
The Germans . The British

THE BATTLE OF MESSINES   50
The witch's cauldron . Final preparations . Pillars of fire . Concrete crypts . Bellevue
Gegenstoss . Scene of a famous fight . Not so friendly fire . Take two

AFTERMATH   86
The zenith of siege warfare . Passchendaele

THE BATTLEFIELD TODAY   92

FURTHER READING   94

INDEX   95

The Western Front June 1917: context of the Flanders offensive

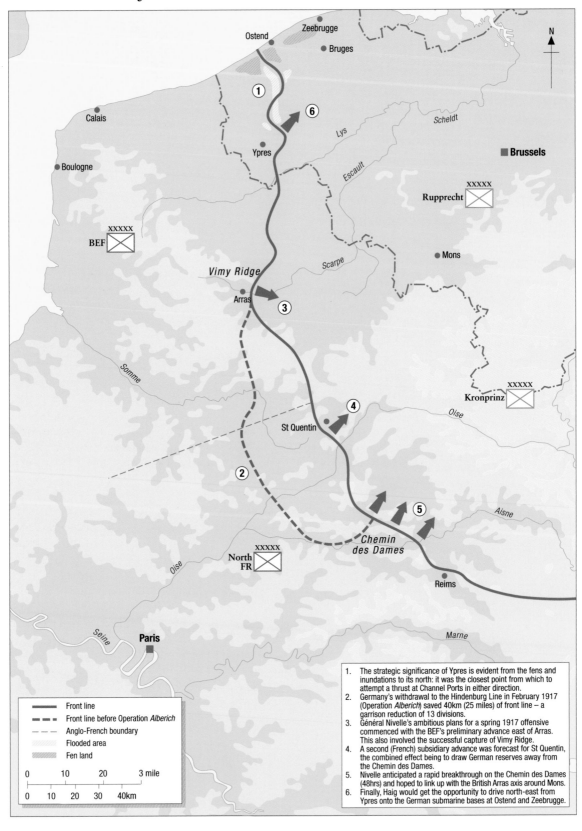

Legend:

— Front line
--- Front line before Operation *Alberich*
– – – Anglo-French boundary
▨ Flooded area
▨ Fen land

0 10 20 3 mile
0 10 20 30 40km

1. The strategic significance of Ypres is evident from the fens and inundations to its north: it was the closest point from which to attempt a thrust at Channel Ports in either direction.
2. Germany's withdrawal to the Hindenburg Line in February 1917 (Operation *Alberich*) saved 40km (25 miles) of front line – a garrison reduction of 13 divisions.
3. Général Nivelle's ambitious plans for a spring 1917 offensive commenced with the BEF's preliminary advance east of Arras. This also involved the successful capture of Vimy Ridge.
4. A second (French) subsidiary advance was forecast for St Quentin, the combined effect being to draw German reserves away from the Chemin des Dames.
5. Nivelle anticipated a rapid breakthrough on the Chemin des Dames (48hrs) and hoped to link up with the British Arras axis around Mons.
6. Finally, Haig would get the opportunity to drive north-east from Ypres onto the German submarine bases at Ostend and Zeebrugge.

ORIGINS OF THE CAMPAIGN

There was a tremble and a swaying of the ground; then a shudder. The sentry…
was hurled against the revetment. Another was thrown over the breastworks.
Dugouts collapsed, burying and crushing those inside. Suddenly we were
enveloped in darkness and the air was full of soil and dust. From the skies
came huge clods of earth, timber, wire pickets, human limbs and whole bodies;
everything swirling in confusion. Trenches are flattened by the falling mass.
Those who cannot dig themselves out are suffocated. The English have
exploded a mine!
*Leutnant Wollinsky, 126th Infantry Regiment, quoted in German Official
History,* Der Weltkrieg 1914–18, *1939*

To anyone familiar with the history of the Western Front, Ypres warrants no
introduction. One could say it is Britain's Verdun: an enduring symbol of
both pluck and futility; the battered spires of 'Wipers' at first analogous to the
dogged spirit of British resistance, then the rallying point for 'Passchendaele'
– an unforgivably costly brawl mired in the sucking quagmire of rain-swept
Flanders. History thrives on such rich contrast but at the time it was not seen
as a play in two acts.

Generations later, it is easy to forget that the Great War was viewed by its
protagonists as one of national survival. But for the unprecedented excesses
of Nazi aggression 20 years later, this perspective may have endured. Britain
and France believed they were fighting for democratic freedoms.

In that context, Ypres had undoubted symbolism; its defence early in the
war spawned the British propaganda mantra 'thus far and no farther'.
Nevertheless, Ypres also held practical strategic significance, primarily as a
hinge for efforts to capture Channel ports – logistic lifelines to both sides. In
the German offensives of October 1914 and April 1915, they were trying to
reach Calais; the British had their eyes constantly on Ostend. The ground
north of Ypres was unsuitable for offensive operations: either flooded by
defenders or a patchwork of fens and dunes. British planners dreamed up
daring amphibious endeavours to bypass the Flanders battlefields but they
never proved sufficiently practical to be worthy of the gamble. Thus Ypres
became the nearest viable avenue of attack.

Unfortunately for the manoeuvrists, the Great War imposed a different
reality and Ypres came to epitomize the largely static, attritional nature of
that conflict. Unlike many other areas of the Western Front, it saw perennially
intense fighting. The Germans surrounded Ypres on three sides – known in
military terminology as a 'salient' – occupying the heights around it like

Baluchi infantry from the British
Indian Army defending
Wytschaete in October 1914.
The Ypres Salient was created
by the BEF's stubborn refusal
to give up the city in the early
months of the war.
(IWM Q 60749)

'schoolboys standing round the edge of a pond plopping stones into the water' – a simile conjured by the oral historian Lyn Macdonald.

'Heights' is a relative term; this network of ridges less than 100m (330ft) above sea level has sarcastically been termed 'Les Alpes de Flandres'. However, in a battle over flat terrain, the advantage gained by such slender increases in altitude could prove decisive. The stones to which Lyn Macdonald refers were of course artillery shells and infantry were employed to either capture or defend advantageous positions for observation parties. Hence the war around Ypres became a rarified struggle for individual positions that in a peaceful landscape might even go unnoticed.

However, at the southern end of the salient lay a feature much more unambiguous. Bulging back out towards British lines in a gentle arc approximately 12km (7 miles) long was the German-occupied Messines Ridge, 85m (280ft) at his highest point and perfectly situated to dominate approaches to the salient as well as avenues of exploitation for any British offensive action to the east. Control of Messines Ridge was a precondition of any breakout from Ypres.

Militarily it was an imperfect position; the German front line sat on a forward slope overlooked by British gunners and rear positions were disadvantaged by a concave gradient, making it difficult to achieve mutual support. But this was Flanders and such considerations were subordinated by the obvious benefits Messines Ridge afforded. British planners coveted it and schemes for its capture were hatched from the very earliest days of the salient's formation.

Despite the caveats applied to Messines's defensive credentials, it was still a daunting undertaking for assaulting infantry: an uphill axis with enemy machine guns in defilade positions, backed up by artillery firing from dead ground beyond. In early 1915, the British Expeditionary Force (BEF) was already learning that without innovation, defeat at Messines would be a foregone conclusion.

There were many lines of development during this period, principally in the realm of indirect fire weapons: artillery and mortars. Artillery was the most obvious solution – it had been breaching defences and softening up the opposition for centuries. But there were other ideas. Britain formed the 'Landships' Committee in February 1915 and within seven months had developed a working prototype of what was later to become the tank. Then there were the mines. The predominance of firepower was driving combatants below ground anyway – it was a logical step.

We will chart the emergence and ascendancy of mine warfare in later chapters. Suffice it to say for now that no one side can reasonably lay claim to it as a genuine innovation. Undermining (digging beneath enemy fortifications and then burning props to create subsidence) was a technique employed from Ancient Egypt through to medieval times. The invention of gunpowder made the tactic all the more dynamic and explosive mines were a feature of the Crimean War and American Civil War of the mid-19th century. During the Russo-Japanese War of 1904–05 – in many ways a preview of the Great War – mining played a decisive role in the siege of Port Arthur.

Australian tunnellers outside a completed dugout project on Hill 63. Tunnellers were hardy souls drawn from a host of underground trades. You would have been ill advised to make an enemy of that 'Digger' on the right. (IWM E 4487)

Pre-war military engineers across Europe were cognizant of mining's niche potential. Observers had witnessed Port Arthur and conducted their own trials. The British Army had a 1910 manual entitled *Military Engineering: Mining and Demolitions*. However, none of this was supported by formal establishment of permanent mining units. Nobody foresaw siege warfare on such a massive scale. Consequently, when trench deadlock ensued, initial attempts at mining were opportunistic, localized and shallow. In December 1914, the Germans were the first to make successful 'blows' (as mine attacks came to be known); retaliation by their opponents soon followed. Techniques improved and expanded rapidly, as did the ambition for these projects. The parochial grapple for knolls at Ypres became a showcase.

Britain's mining effort was championed by an extraordinary man we shall be returning to: Sir John Norton-Griffiths, surely the embodiment of the Edwardian spirit. His energy and self-belief was limitless. Within months of establishing small specialist mining units in the Ypres sector, Norton-Griffiths had his eyes on Messines Ridge. When the British started to achieve significant depth in early summer 1915, Norton-Griffiths and his disciples knew that 'earthquaking the ridge' (as they put it) was now a practicable venture. Having secured the approval of the BEF's Engineer-in-Chief, Brigadier-General George Fowke, they submitted a formal application for

The spires of Ypres viewed from the German front line south-west of St Eloi. This photograph illustrates how commanding their position up on Messines Ridge was. (Author's collection)

their ever-expanding scheme in November 1915. It was approved by General Headquarters (GHQ) the following February, shortly after a fellow exponent of mining, Brigadier-General Robert Harvey, had been appointed as the first BEF 'Inspector of Mines'. Typically for Norton-Griffiths, he had started the work beneath Messines Ridge regardless. Tunnelling – as it came to be known – was a painstaking business and the earliest they would be ready to deliver any of their blows would be the summer of 1916.

Laudable as these subterranean aspirations were, blasting the German front line at Messines stood less chance of reaching fruition as an end in itself. It needed to be harnessed to conventional military objectives. Field Marshal Sir Douglas Haig, the BEF Commander-in-Chief, had always favoured Flanders as the best place to unlock the Western Front. Thinking at the strategic level, he agreed with the British Admiralty that German submarine activity in Ostend and Zeebrugge posed a grave threat to Channel shipping lanes. Soon after assuming command, Haig bid the Fourth Army commander, General Sir Henry Rawlinson, to work up a plan to clear the Belgian coastline by thrusting north-east from Ypres.

Straightening the salient amounted to a series of cascading preconditions. First you had to capture Messines Ridge to create a 'defensive flank'; thence over Pilckem Ridge and the Steenbeek (River) to bring guns onto German depth defences at Passchendaele. Beyond was open country. Messines Ridge fell within the sector allocated to Second Army, commanded by General Sir Herbert Plumer.

1 Second Army's capture of Messines Ridge was the obvious prerequisite for the entire Ypres undertaking; from it the Germans could retain a) a clear view of troop concentrations massing for the attack on the northern axis and b) the ability to dominate that axis as it progressed north-east.
2 Originally, Plumer was in favour of taking Messines in three 24-hour phases. This was later truncated to one day. Note that exploitation from Messines was not planned for at this stage.
3 Both Rawlinson and Plumer concurred that the northern assault should take place at least one day later and concentrate on consolidating the limited objective of Pilckem Ridge before pushing further east.

4 Haig believed it would be possible to reach Langemarck and Zonnebeke on the first day (albeit in four distinct phases) *simultaneous* to both the attack on Messines…
5 … and the centre, broadening axis, which was intended to be achieved through the application of massed armour. However, the plan was later abandoned due to a) shortages of machines and b) the eventual (7 May) decision to treat Messines as a distinct preliminary operation.
6 Irrespective, all parties concurred that the eventual aim of the offensive was to break out north-east around the Houthulst Forest and strike for Ostend.

The Ypres Salient

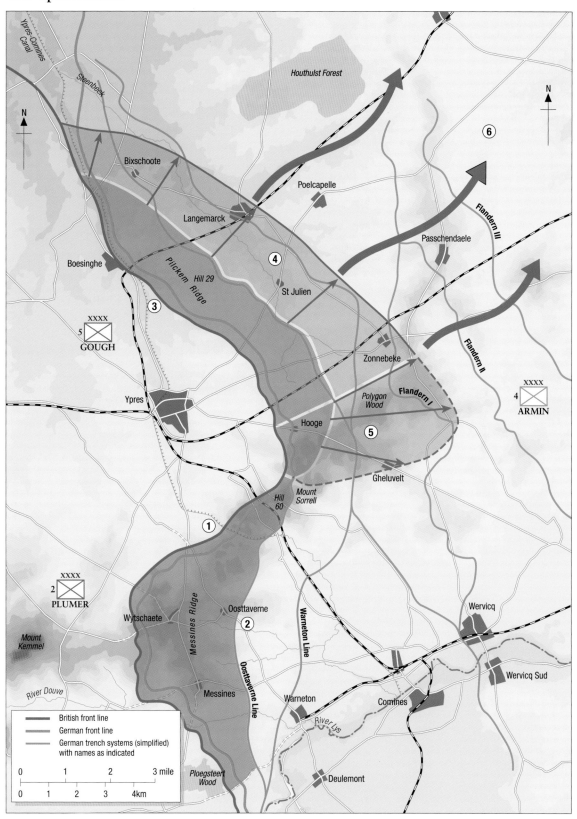

Houthulst Forest

Ypres-Comines Canal

Steenbeek

N

Bixschoote

Poelcapelle

Langemarck

④

Passchendaele

Boesinghe

Pickem Ridge

Hill 29

St Julien

③

Flandern III

XXXX
5
GOUGH

Ypres

Zonnebeke

Polygon Wood

Flandern I

Flandern II

XXXX
4
ARMIN

N

⑥

Hooge

⑤

Gheluvelt

Hill 60

Mount Sorrell

①

Mount Kemmel

XXXX
2
PLUMER

Messines Ridge

Oosttaverne

②

Warneton Line

Wervicq

Wytschaete

Oosttaverne Line

Wervicq Sud

River Douve

Messines

Warneton

Comines

River Lys

Deulemont

Ploegsteert Wood

British front line
German front line
German trench systems (simplified) with names as indicated

0   1   2   3 mile
0   1   2   3   4km

A practice 'blow' at the Aubigny Mine School in May 1916. Mines designed to crater the surface were classified as 'over-charged' – apt given the staggering quantities of explosive involved. (IWM Q 572)

General Sir Tom Bridges, then a major-general in command of 19th Division, IX Corps, Second Army, later described Plumer as 'the Cinderella of the [BEF] Army Commanders'; the Ypres Salient being 'his unsavoury kitchen'. Plumer had a mixed relationship with Haig, who deemed him to be too cautious. For his part Plumer was older and more 'senior' than Haig. Gossip has it that once Plumer had given him a weak score when instructing at Staff College.

Such is the politics of institutions. But the tension is important because many historians believe that Plumer was not given sufficient influence on Haig's Ypres offensive. A strident advocate of 'bite and hold' operations with limited objectives, Plumer acted as a brake on Haig's dreams of rapid breakout. He argued that after Messines there should be a pause for consolidation before pressing ahead with the primary northern axis. Allied relationships soon complicated such a unitary view of the war's prosecution; the Germans had attacked at Verdun, which in turn forced the 'joint' Anglo-French Somme offensive of summer 1916. There were no resources for Flanders.

Nevertheless, Haig had a chance to sell his plans again at the Allied Chantilly Conference in November 1916, which sought to agree plans for the following year. He arrived armed with a directive from the War Cabinet in London that there was 'no greater importance than the expulsion of the enemy from the Belgian coast'. It was agreed that Flanders would form the cornerstone of BEF's contribution for 1917.

In the New Year, Général Joffre, the French Commander-in-Chief, was replaced by Nivelle, a dynamic and aggressive soldier with confident ideas. He initiated a joint spring offensive whereby the French would attack at the Chemin Des Dames with a subsidiary preliminary push by the BEF at Arras, aimed at drawing off German theatre reserves. Swept up by the cavalier atmosphere Nivelle generated, Haig suggested a more vigorous timetable for Ypres. The German withdrawal to the newly constructed Siegfried Stellung (known to the British as the Hindenburg Line) in February 1917 appeared to vindicate this mood of optimism.

Plumer stood firm, as his biographer believes, 'clearly determined that lives should not be wasted without due cause'. When asked to comment, Rawlinson backed Plumer for the most part, agreeing that there must be a pause after the capture of Messines Ridge. Haig overruled them both and his personal corrections were absorbed into the Macmullen Memorandum – GHQ's formal operational directive. The whole offensive was to be mounted simultaneously, at a month's notice on the heels of Nivelle's forecast gains. Disappointed with Plumer and Rawlinson's apparent timidity, he then selected the young (47-year-old) cavalryman General Sir Hubert Gough to command the northern axis – his main effort. Plumer retained responsibility for Messines Ridge.

Yet the convoluted saga of Haig's plans had one more twist to take. The audacious Général Nivelle's April Chemin des Dames offensive failed at great human cost, despite an initially sound contribution from the BEF at Arras. Nivelle was replaced by Général Pétain and the Allied leaders convened in Paris for a somewhat subdued conference in early May. The mood was dark. One week previously, French troops had started to commit 'acts of collective indiscipline' in protest at the folly of the Chemin des Dames. Allied shipping losses to Germany's submarine fleet during April 1917 had reached record levels. The United States had entered the war on 6 April but would not be ready to contribute anytime soon. Pressure had to be maintained on Germany and only Britain was in a position to do so. The Prime Minister, David Lloyd George sealed that promise by asserting that 'the enemy must not be left in peace for one moment'.

Haig briefed his army commanders on 7 May. Evidently, the gravity of the Allies' predicament had left an impression on him, as had Pétain's insistence on 'action in breadth [attrition] rather than depth [manoeuvre]'. In apparent contradiction to previous direction, Haig declared that 'the objective of the French and British will now be to wear down and exhaust the enemy's resistance by systematically attacking him by surprise'. Pressure would be maintained on the Arras front and, in the clearest sign that he had backtracked, the offensive scheme for Ypres was amended one final time. Messines Ridge would be attacked as a distinct preliminary operation; the northern main effort would occur 'some weeks later'. Haig approached Plumer at the start of the conference and asked him when he could be ready to tackle Messines Ridge. Plumer and the tunnellers had not sat idle. His reply, without pause: 'Today, one month, Sir' – 7 June.

CHRONOLOGY

1914

3 August   German cavalry patrols enter Belgium at the spearhead of an invading army.

August   Battles of Mons, Ardennes and Le Cateau as the BEF and French try to stem the German advance into Belgium and France.

September   Allied counterattacks on the Marne, Artois and Aisne drive the Germans back.

October   The struggle for manoeuvre culminates in the battle for Ypres. The hasty defences from Switzerland to the Channel ports solidify through the winter.

1915

March   British offensive at Neuve Chapelle. Failure attributed to 'poor communication'.

April   Germans initiate second battle of Ypres. Poisonous gas used for the first time.

May   British attack at Aubers Ridge and Festubert to no avail while French launch the costly second battle of Artois north of Arras.

September to October   British offensive at Loos. First use of the 'creeping barrage'. Battle of Artois continues with a subsidiary French effort east of Reims. Initial success soon gives way to impasse.

November   Sir John Norton-Griffith's Messines Ridge mining scheme submitted to GHQ.

December   Haig replaces Field Marshal French in command of BEF.

1916

January	Messines mining scheme approved by GHQ.
February	Germans attempt to draw the French into unsustainable attritional battle by attacking at Verdun. It grinds on bloody and indecisive through to June.
July	In part to relieve pressure on the French, the British launch their offensive on the Somme. Negligible gains came at horrendous cost but Germany persuaded to suspend Verdun offensive. Falkenhayn replaced in command of German forces by Hindenburg and Ludendorff.
July to September	Somme offensive continues with attacks at Delville Wood, Pozières and Thiepval.
October	French counterattack at Verdun.
November	Battle of Somme concluded after battle of Ancre. Gains of just 11km (7 miles) no consolation for 500,000 casualties. Germans lose 420,000. Allied Chantilly Conference convened to discuss plans for 1917.
December	At Verdun, the French finally drive the Germans back to where they started. Général Joffre replaced at head of French Army by Général Nivelle.

1917

February	Gross manning pressures compel German withdrawal to Siegfried Stellung (Hindenburg Line). Calais Agreement between Haig and Nivelle on shape of the year's offensive operations.
April	America enters the war. Allied joint spring offensive. British attack astride the river Scarpe at Arras. Some spectacular gains, including Vimy Ridge, but pause called after a week. The French effort at the Chemin des Dames makes encouraging early progress but falters after heavy losses.
4 May	Second Allied Conference in Paris. The Chemin des Dames having ended in failure, French suffer acts of 'mutiny' and Nivelle is replaced by Pétain. Haig cleared to mount Flanders offensive.
7 May	Haig sets date for Messines Ridge preliminary operation: 7 June.
21 May	Preparatory barrage opens.
31 May	Preparatory barrage intensifies.
7 June	Battle of Messines commences with detonation of 19 mines.

8–11 June	Second Army (principally II ANZAC) fights to finalize gains.
14 June	After German Fourth Army withdrawal to reserve lines, Messines battle is concluded.
31 July	Third battle of Ypres (Passchendaele) is launched. Gough's early August debacles at Gheluvelt Plateau, Langemarck and St Julien are improved by Plumer's judicious limited operations like Polygon Wood in September. However, having bogged in a rainy quagmire, both Britain and Germany suffer terrible casualties – 400,000 versus 348,000. The offensive is brought to a close in November.
20 November	Tank attack launched at Cambrai with stunning initial successes. German Second Army launches its successful counterattack ten days later after BEF exhausts itself on Bourlon Wood.
2 December	In the wake of revolution, Russia withdraws from the war under the Treaty of Brest-Litovsk.

1918

March	Germans open the offensive on the Somme, making huge gains but exhausting their logistic capabilities.
April	German subsidiary offensive in Flanders fails as the buttress of Ypres holds firm.
May	After a diversionary attack west of the Chemin des Dames, Germany throws itself once more at the French. The biggest advances since 1914 see the Germans pressing against the river Marne once more but overextended forces are checked with the assistance of fresh US divisions.
June to July	Further German offensives lack the impetus of early efforts and result in withdrawals.
August	Allied counterattacks commence across the entire front. Spent German forces are soon in full retreat. Ludendorff dubs 8 August – the battle of Amiens – his 'black day'.
September	Germans have been driven back to their start point on the Siegfried Stellung by the end of the month. US forces make significant gains south-east of Verdun.
October	BEF, French and US armies press home concerted, coordinated offensives across the entire Western Front, breaching German defensive lines routinely. British First Army reaches Mons.
11 November	Armistice is signed and the Germans agree to pull back east of the Rhine within 14 days.

OPPOSING COMMANDERS

PLAYING THE HAND THAT'S DEALT

Debate among the architects of Ypres is illustrative of the enormous doctrinal pressures imposed by the Great War. It would be easy to denigrate Haig in this instance, arguing that Plumer's circumspection was vindicated by French failures at the Chemin des Dames, the chimera of breakthrough a misguided illusion. Yet too often the grand strategic equation is overlooked in study of the Great War. Haig and his French counterparts were under sustained political pressure to end the slaughter; both Britain and France remained functioning democracies. Britain's wealth – and war effort – depended on the shipping lanes that were threatened by German submarines. The clock ticked and the war's outcome was no foregone conclusion.

Regrettably, the unprecedented nature of conflict at the front made grand designs the preserve of hope over experience. Whether or not Great War leaders accepted the fact, it was, during the middle years at least, essentially a war of attrition that would be settled by weight of bloodshed and long-term economic blockade.

It is important to reflect on the unprecedented circumstances military leaders were presented with. As I have stressed in two previous Campaign titles about the Great War, these men had started their careers in armies that still bore resemblance to Napoleonic forebears: muzzle-loading artillery, infantry fighting in line with single-shot weapons and garish uniforms. With hindsight, the auguries are clearly in evidence by 1914; at the time it was less obvious. Nevertheless, nobody disputes that the next four years were truly revolutionary. Crushingly, advances were not uniform; armies could kill better than they could communicate. Manoeuvre was, as we have already seen, a relative term. Prescriptive planning and topographical fixation became symptoms of this malaise.

Far from being Luddite, some innovative generals on both sides assimilated this transformation with remarkable dexterity, harnessing emerging technologies on the one hand and old ideas – like mining – on the other. 1917 was a seminal year.

Yet field commanders who grasped the ground realities were often insulated from the political ones. Careful schemes and strictly limited objectives may have reduced casualties – and thus attract plaudits today – but they also demanded a patience from politicians and populations that modern society would probably exhaust before a brigade had moved a

An approachable and considerate man, General Sir Herbert 'Daddy' Plumer (foreground) won the affection of his troops but also their respect: he was highly competent. Haig would later call on him to try and rescue the fortunes of Third Ypres. (IWM Q 23665)

kilometre. Limited objectives meant limited gains; thus battle-winning strategies were not necessarily war-winning ones, even cumulatively. Comprehending these complexities from a contemporary standpoint is hard enough; conquering them at the time was nigh-on impossible.

THE BRITISH

General Sir Herbert Plumer

History has not been generous to Plumer; our media world would doubtless be even more dismissive. Aged 60 in 1917, he appears to be the perfect caricature for an out-of-touch 'chateau general': Old Etonian, top heavy, white moustache and ruddy, pippin-cheeked countenance. Even at the time, some disparaged his avuncular manner as ineffectual or imbecilic. But the trap is apt. Appearances were deceptive.

Far from being detached, Plumer was a compassionate leader with a 'common touch'. A private in the Highland Light Infantry recalls that Plumer 'was a great man; just a little fellow… but he was a fine man to speak to, not a bit standoffish. He spoke to all ranks.'[1] Anthony Eden (Prime Minister of Britain 1955–57) served under Plumer in Second Army. He wrote: 'at a superficial glance, Plumer might not be impressive but watch his methods for a while or hear him speak and you would know that here was a skilled and painstaking commander'.[2] His eye for detail was notorious, though applied without being prescriptive to subordinates. Plumer's modest staff of 50 was drilled with the mantra 'trust, training and thoroughness' and pressed always to consider themselves as 'servants of the infantry'.

An infantryman by trade, Plumer cut his teeth in British colonial campaigns like Sudan and the Matabele Rebellion in Rhodesia, also serving with distinction under Colonel Baden-Powell in the South African War at the turn of the century. His operational record in the Great War started when he was promoted to lieutenant-general in command of V Corps in January 1915. Plumer's deft handling of that formation during the second battle of Ypres in April 1915 earned him command of Second Army that May.

The corps commanders

Plumer employed three of his four corps for the Messines operation. In the north was X Corps, commanded by Lieutenant-General Sir Thomas Morland since 1915. Morland was another distinguished colonial soldier, for his part in Nigeria where he rose to become Inspector General of the West African Field Force, mobilized to deter French incursions. On formation of the BEF in 1914, Morland was placed at the helm of the 5th Infantry Division, a regular 'Old Contemptible' formation.

Lieutenant-General Sir Alexander Hamilton-Gordon held the centre with IX Corps. Grandson of the mid-19th-century British Prime Minister, Hamilton-Gordon started his career with service in the Second Afghan War of 1878–80, later returning to British India as Director of Military Operations. He saw out the initial stages of the Great War in India and then as Commandant of Aldershot Garrison in Britain until being appointed to IX Corps on promotion in late 1916.

1. Lyn Macdonald, *They called it Passchendaele*, 1978
2. Anthony Eden, *Another World 1897–1917*, 1976

Second Australian and New Zealand Army Corps (II ANZAC) completes the trio. At Messines it was commanded by Lieutenant-General Sir Alexander Godley, a British professional soldier. It was not uncommon for 'Dominion' troops to have British commanders at this level. His association with Australasia came in 1910 when Lord Kitchener dispatched him to command the New Zealand Army as a major-general. He raised and trained the New Zealand Expeditionary Force in 1914 and then commanded the combined New Zealand and Australian Division at Gallipoli in 1915. An amusing postscript to Godley's career is that he commanded an infantry platoon in the 1940 Home Guard! His company commander must have felt a little underqualified.

THE GERMANS

Senior German officers also had creative differences – plenty are documented – but their fluid *Gruppe* system engendered a less dogmatic and hierarchical atmosphere to battlefield command. On first impression, it seems bizarre that the exacting Prussian military culture should produce such a pragmatic policy but it too is commonly misunderstood.

The underlying principle of the *Gruppe* system was that formal structures were of secondary importance to the value of situational awareness. Consequently, a commander arriving at the battlefront at the head of his reserve formation may well take orders from a more junior officer with superior grasp of events. This was a principle that applied even when the senior man was subverted by three grades. Commanders were encouraged to apply *Fingerspitzengefühl* – a combination of experience and visceral instinct – in pursuit of timely decisions, and create conditions for others to do so.

General Sixt von Armin – one of Germany's most able Great War field commanders. He went on to earn an oak leaf cluster to his Pour le Mérite and was given full military honours at his funeral in 1936. (Author's collection)

The *Gruppe* system also applied to task organization. Corps headquarters were given a geographic area of responsibility (which created local familiarity) and re-titled, for instance, Gruppe Arras. Then various subordinate divisions could come in and out of the line on a flexible basis. The system also enabled ad hoc formations to be marshalled amid the chaos of battle, maximizing the utility of decimated units and piecemeal reinforcements.

General der Infanterie Sixt von Armin
Germany's overall commander in Flanders was General Sixt von Armin, a long-serving professional infantry soldier with a stellar record of generalship in the Great War. Emerging from the Franco-Prussian War with severe wounds and an Iron Cross, Armin was also very experienced on the staff, reaching *General der Infanterie* as Director of the Joint Warfare Department. At the outbreak of war, he was in command of IV Corps and led them with distinction at Arras, Loretto Heights and La Bassée in 1915 and then the Somme in 1916, for which he was awarded Germany's foremost Great War decoration the Pour le Mérite (often nicknamed the 'Blue Max' in honour of fighter ace recipients). Command of Fourth Army (Flanders) came in 1917, just in time to meet the British Ypres offensive.

General der Kavallerie Maximilian von Laffert
General von Laffert commanded Gruppe Wytschaete, the formation with responsibility for Messines Ridge. His official appointment was XIX (2nd Royal Saxon) Army Corps, which he had shepherded through the

Marne in 1914, La Bassée alongside Armin in 1915 and then also the Somme and the Lys (in Flanders) in 1916. He too received a Blue Max for his efforts on the Somme before being posted to Flanders.

Of noble birth, Laffert had started his career as an infantryman in 1874 but transferred into the Hussars two years later. His service record was strongly weighted in favour of cavalry field command and he endured precious little purgatory as a cog in Germany's staff machine. It betrays the nature of warfare on the Western Front that a man with such rich experience of cavalry soldiering should end his career from whence he came: in command of infantry.

OPPOSING FORCES

THE GERMANS

Operation *Alberich* – Germany's withdrawal to the Siegfried Stellung in February 1917 – was a straightforward response to the crushing losses inflicted on the German Army the previous year. Failure to defeat France in the first months of the war had necessitated a broadly defensive posture on the Western Front while Germany and its allies concentrated on Russia. Nevertheless, the decision to 'bleed France dry' at Verdun in 1916 had proved double edged and Germany's stubborn intolerance of territorial retirement led to extravagant counterattacks whenever the French and British made gains. The number of German casualties on the Somme surprises people accustomed to tales of British slaughter; Germany's total for the Western Front in 1916 exceeded 750,000. Whereas the Entente powers could draw on the reserves of empire, Germany's population was blockaded and dwindling.

By occupying the carefully constructed Siegfried Stellung, the Germans saved 40km (25 miles) of front line. In manning terms, this equated to 13 infantry divisions – a good working figure to raise a viable theatre reserve. However, they had already created a false economy by reducing the manpower establishment of an infantry division. Of the 157 divisions in theatre only 52 had avoided battle that year and many of those were inexperienced or made up of older (*Landwehr*) troops.

Contemporary British intelligence reports were citing the reduced physique of prisoners and claiming a marked fall in morale. In June 1917, one assessed that Germany was 'now within four to six months of a date at which she will be unable to maintain the strength of her units in the field'.[3]

GHQ's intelligence analysts were right about Germany's parlous manpower situation. The spare capacity created by Operation *Alberich* was soon to be consumed by the imperative to shore up the Italian front. Respite would not come until Russia's capitulation in October; nobody knew this yet. But optimistic judgements about morale proved hasty. The *Feldgrauen* were a stoic breed and had plenty of fight left.

It was a question of making do. Reduced infantry establishments brought a division's strength down from six regiments to three, each regiment containing three battalions of infantry. The basic building block of a battalion was its four companies – the smallest entity capable of independent action,

3. Quoted in British Official History, *Messines and Third Ypres 1917*, Brig. Gen. Sir James Edmonds, 1948

A *Pionier* field engineer survey section mapping trenches at St Eloi. Beset by acute manpower shortages in 1917, Germany maximized their fighting power by shortening the line and applying clever defensive doctrine. (IWM Q 45586)

particularly in defence. Officially, a German infantry company mustered 264 men but by this stage of the war they would be fortunate to feed two-thirds of that number.

The German Army made up for this adroitly, first of all, through exceptional junior leadership. The ethos of decentralized *Fingerspitzengefühl* gave junior officers the latitude to make senior decisions. In his eloquent account of Great War German infantry soldiering, *Storm of Steel*, Ernst Jünger attests to the tenacity and initiative of these commanders.

Infantry battalions in the line were issued a high concentration of machine guns, the keystone of any defensive position: eight water-cooled Maxims in their integral machine-gun company, augmented by specialist detachments of expert gunners trained and employed at divisional level. The company commander had up to six (though usually less) of the 08/15 model 'light' Maxim guns, stripped of their stable but cumbersome sledge mounts and therefore suitable for more rapid relocation.

1916 had taught the Germans valuable lessons about the most economical way to man trench systems, most notably the folly of placing too many men in vulnerable front lines. This gave rise to an entirely novel approach to defensive doctrine that will be detailed in the Opposing plans chapter. In sum, their emphasis was switched from positional defence to counterattack. Placing faith in smaller, machine-gun-equipped units made survivability paramount.

To this end (indeed throughout the war), Germany invested serious thought into the design of fighting positions. German engineers did not invent

German engineers perfected the use of reinforced concrete to build pillboxes so solid that they remain – indomitable – on the Flanders landscape to this day. This example is east of Messines. (Author's collection)

reinforced concrete but they certainly perfected its martial applications. With a high water table and shattered drainage system, the Flanders battlefield was not conducive to deep dugouts of the like found in chalk redoubts further south. Here reinforced concrete really came into its own, allowing construction of blockhouses, artillery emplacements and machine-gun nests *above* ground. Though camouflaged with turfs, incessant shelling soon stripped them bare, earning these bleached, squat structures the moniker 'pillboxes'. Studding the landscape, many sit around Ypres, stout as ever, 90 years on.

It was the impregnability of German bunkers – and the murderous fields of fire reaped by the Maxims within – that bid tunnellers to burrow beneath Flanders. Otherwise only a direct hit by heavy howitzers could destroy them. Nonetheless, it is important to concede that German military engineers, known as *Pioniere*, were the first to adopt mining successfully and no exposition of the Great War's subterranean struggle can take a single nation's perspective.

MINE WARFARE

Alert readers will have noticed a contradiction in the narrative: Britain's mining offensive at Messines was made possible by achieving deep galleries yet the high water table in Flanders is credited with preventing German engineers from constructing the deep *Stellungen* favoured elsewhere. Mine warfare was first and foremost a battle against geology – an unremitting foe at the best of times. When Britain gained the upper hand against this third party, it was the turning point in the underground war.

In cross section, Messines Ridge is a geological trifle pudding. Beneath shallow topsoil is soft sandy clay, workable but moist. Below that is a 15m (50ft) band of so-called 'Kemmel Sand' – *Schwimmsand* to the Germans – a miner's nightmare. Sandwiched between firmer layers, this slurry behaves like pressurized quicksand, effectively flooding any shaft sunk into it. Once through the Kemmel, one reaches a deep band of blue clay that is firm, albeit with a high degree of plasticity (expansion) on contact with oxygen.

Tentative forays below ground in the winter of 1914–15 were shallow – 5m (16ft) or less. More significant projects demanded depth and a commensurate

LEFT

Pioniere taking a breath of fresh air at a shafthead. Unlike the autonomous British tunnelling companies they dug against, German mining units rotated out of the line with parent infantry divisions. This proved disadvantageous. (RE Museum 23/256/143)

LEFT

Pioniere taking a breath of fresh air at a shafthead. Unlike the autonomous British tunnelling companies they dug against, German mining units rotated out of the line with parent infantry divisions. This proved disadvantageous. (RE Museum 23/256/143)

RIGHT

Sir John Norton-Griffiths attracted the sobriquet 'Empire Jack'. It is easy to understand why: he was a patriotic man of extraordinary talent and energy. Even this sketch betrays it. (By kind permission of the National Portrait Gallery)

uplift in expertise. Many enthusiastic amateurs in the hastily cobbled-together BEF 'Brigade Mining Sections' and German *Stollenbau* companies had prior experience of civilian mines but rarely mastery of survey, infrastructure and rescue. They were certainly not going to crack the Kemmel problem.

The Germans were mildly complacent about this and did not see fit to alter the establishment of existing *Festungbataillone* and the *Pionier* companies within. Although they recruited specialists, military mining remained wedded to mainstream engineering structures until May 1916. Without elite status, *Pioniere* were abused and misused, much to the exasperation of their commanders – and to the detriment of underground work.

Perhaps what they needed was a man of similar energy and vision as Sir John Norton-Griffiths, surely the progenitor of Britain's mining capability in the Great War. His curriculum vitae reads like a 'Who's Who' of late Victorian heroes: command of native scouts in the Matabele War, Earl Roberts' bodyguard during the South African War, Member of Parliament, Director of Arsenal Football Club, founder member of the Royal British Legion, entrepreneur and noted civil engineer. In 1914, Norton-Griffiths raised and equipped a cavalry regiment at his own expense.

He took up the banner of 'tunnelling' with messianic zeal, providing in the first instance 'clay-kickers' from his own civil engineering firm. Ypres clay was almost identical to that found beneath London and Manchester, where Norton-Griffiths had been building sewers and underground railways. Using the token rank of major, he toured BEF units in his own Rolls-Royce with a boot full of spirits to break the ice. Miners being tough and reliable men, commanders were reluctant to give them up. But the force of Norton-Griffiths' personality won through. His obituary describes someone 'vehement and theatrical as a speaker... his meetings were often rowdy'.[4] Staff officers recall how he would push the furniture aside and demonstrate clay-kicking techniques on the floor.

4. Royal Engineers Museum Collection

In Norton-Griffiths' wake strode a man of great efficiency: Colonel (later Major-General) Napier Harvey. He created the infrastructure necessary to accommodate such rapid expansion of British tunnelling. Although miners transferred from the infantry, plenty more were extracted direct from civilian mines and, such was the urgency, arrived at the front with only a few days of military training. Captain Grant Grieve recalls that 'their first salutes induced apoplexy in a passing Sergeant Major'.[5] Many older men came forward, some beyond the official limit, but allowances were made; above all else tunnelling demanded a cool head. Everyone was a volunteer and, as skilled and hazardous work, tunnelling attracted a rate of pay six times that of an infantry private.

By July 1916, there were 33 BEF tunnelling companies, with up to 550 men in each. The majority (25) came from Britain, nicknamed 'Moles'. From December 1915, they were joined by 'Beavers' from Canada (3), and 'Diggers' from Australia (4) and New Zealand (1). All underground trades had a look-in: coal, tin, copper and gold miners, sewer men, etc. *Pioniere* were drawn mainly from the coal mines and their numbers diminished later in the war when Germany was forced to address raw material shortages.

BEF tunnelling companies were issued a geographic sector whereas *Pionier* companies moved with the division to which they were attached. Operational security rendered mine warfare an extremely secretive business; hence there are few diaries and photographic images. All staff work was strictly classified.

A tunnelling project required four preconditions: a worthwhile objective, fixed, within reach and through a suitable medium. The first point may seem

This inclined shafthead (left) was situated on Hill 70 at Lens. Inclines were favoured for the shallow workings prevalent early in the mining campaign but, in most cases, deeper projects demanded a vertical shaft. It is evident from this photograph how easy it was to disguise shaftheads as normal dugouts; spoil was another matter. (IWM E 1712)

5. *Tunnellers*, Captain W. Grant Grieve, 1936

self-evident but as the mine warfare historian Peter Barton puts it, many early enterprises were merely 'devoted to ornamental destruction'.[6] 'Fixed' is also slightly obvious until one considers that troops occupying a trench system reserve the right to withdraw; this was a genuine concern at Messines. Both sides employed geologists on the Western Front (in the first instance to identify sources of drinking water) and their survey work was vital. The rest was down to the tunnellers.

Unless the topography allowed one to cut straight into a hillside, deep mine projects first needed a shaft – either vertical or inclined. In Flanders, the principal challenge here was Kemmel Sand. Eventually, tunnellers overcame this by a process known as 'tubbing' – cylindrical steel or concrete sections dropped into a vertical shaft to prevent ingress of slurry. More sections are added from the top as the stack descends. Once through the Kemmel and into clay, normal timbers sufficed. From their positions higher up, the Germans were disadvantaged and, owing to their exasperation with Kemmel, assumed for a long time that British plans would by stymied by it.

Shaftheads were seldom placed in the front line, even though that meant longer attacks. Enemy raiding parties might discover them and the associated labour activity was less conspicuous in support lines, where work parties ferrying stores and revetment timbers were commonplace. British tunnellers occasionally disguised shaftheads with notices saying 'Danger! Deep Well'.

Having achieved the required depth, it was commonplace to excavate a 'lateral' gallery running parallel to the front line. Laterals had two purposes. They provided redundancy so that compromise or destruction of a 'fighting' tunnel did not necessarily demand a fresh shaft; and they doubled up as a protective mine network.

Blind like the moles they emulated, tunnellers relied on the noise made by enemy workings to foretell an impending blow. Fortunately, sound travels faster through solids than air so they stood a reasonable chance of detecting activity.

6. *Beneath Flanders Fields*, Peter Barton et al., 2004

Tunnellers on both sides were constantly vigilant – many shallower lateral networks were constructed purely for the purpose of listening. In the beginning, tunnellers used stethoscopes. Later, they designed incredibly sensitive devices called geophones. One officer recalls dropping an ant near to his geophone receiver: 'It sounded like an elephant walking around in lead-soled boots'.[7]

Akin to sonar operators in submarine warfare, men honed their skills to the point where they could differentiate the tap of an encroaching pick from dripping of water. Logs from listening posts are remarkably detailed. One British listener beneath Vimy Ridge in June 1916 reported: 'German conversation; two men at winch: "Karl, have you heard from your wife lately?"; "No, she has not written for two weeks"'.[8]

Owing to this imperative for stealth, digging rates were painstakingly slow, sometimes only a metre or so per day. But in the malleable clay beneath Flanders, the British employed a technique that made them both quicker and quieter than their opponents: 'clay-kicking'. In the niche world of tunnelling, it amounted to a secret weapon. Rather than wielding a two-handed 'push pick' at the clay face, the Mole would lie on his back supported by a plank and, manipulating a sharp flat 'grafting' tool with his feet, lever the clay gently away in blocks. Lying on their sides behind him, the other members of the shift would bag the spoil carefully and run it back to the shafthead on rubber-wheeled carts. There the spoil would be raised to the surface by hand windlass and buried in shell holes after dark; blue spoil could easily betray the presence of a tunnel. Enemy airmen and balloon observers were trained to look for it.

The 'fighting' tunnels were economical in size. Unlike civilian ore mining, the purpose was simply to drive forwards to a point where they could excavate a mine chamber for explosives; space was an extravagance. Thus tunnels were approximately 120cm (4 feet) by 60cm (2 feet): the back of an armchair or a large fireplace. When two men needed to pass, one would have to lie down while the other crawled over his back. Despite air pumps operated by 'mates' in support of the 'face-men', it was foul and fetid in the tunnels. Matches burned with just a red glow. Otto Riebike, a German *Pionier* officer, elucidates: 'The heat underground becomes insufferable. The sappers take their jackets off and soon they stand bare-chested like the journeymen of Vulcan in the depths of this dreadful battle. The air becomes thinner and thinner, the length of the galleries is too great for the air pumps'.[9]

Tunnels could run for hundreds of metres; the longest was a 6km (4-mile) lateral at La Bassée. Generally, they were lit by candles (easy to replenish and also useful as a timepiece) and supported by box timbers spaced relative to the risk of collapse. Blue clay was pretty sound but would expand on contact with air, crushing the supports. Tunnellers beneath Ypres learned to space them by a few inches so they could cleave away the encroaching clay periodically.

Structural collapse was just one of the countless perils of warfare below ground – and something civilian miners were familiar with. Flanders also presented the threat of flood from underground rivers and 'alluvials' (ancient riverbeds now forming seams of waterlogged silt). In one staggering incident at Neuve Chapelle in April 1917, a party of Moles was deluged by water flooding in from a German gallery they accidentally encroached upon. Two men escaped; a third had the option to do so but instead tried to shift a spoil

7. Lieutenant Brian Frayling RE, IWM Sound Archive 4105
8. *Tunnellers*, Captain W. Grant Grieve, 1936
9. *Unsere Pioniere im Weltkriege*, Leutnant Otto Riebike et al., 1925 – translated by Col. Jack Sheldon

Proto breathing apparatus looks primitive but it was highly effective when used by trained personnel. Goggles were worn as standard – not evident in this posed shot. The small cage is for his 'tunneller's friends': generally canaries or mice. (IWM E 1683)

trolley trapping the face party. He drowned in the attempt. Facing a watery death, three of the men at the face managed to enter the German system through the breach, found their way to the surface and recovered back across no man's land!

'Chokedamp' – the coal miner's term for carbon monoxide – also stalked the tunnels. Odourless, colourless and tasteless, carbon monoxide kills quickly even in modest concentrations. Survivors attest to a sudden onset of vice-like headaches and rapid loss of coordination. Unconsciousness then led to death. Here early warning was provided by the 'tunneller's friends': canaries, mice and rabbits. Canaries were favoured because they would fall off their perch, this being more obvious than mice and rabbits simply curling up and going to sleep. But it was important to clip their claws; otherwise the little sentinels would cling on. Tunnellers were fond of these quasi-pets. Animals that survived multiple encounters with chokedamp sometimes were given early retirement.

The principal source of carbon monoxide beneath Flanders was camouflet explosions; small charges designed to collapse enemy mine workings. If you add the casualties caused by resulting gas release, camouflets accounted for the majority of deaths underground. Using either torpedo-shaped charges placed with an auger or conventional high explosive packed against the face, tunnellers would try to time camouflets so they coincided with shift changes and then fire a second to trap rescue parties encumbered by 'Proto' breathing apparatus. Proto-trained rescue specialists were a prized asset worth targeting. It took nerve to prime a camouflet, inserting fiddly detonators in the knowledge that the enemy may well have heard your approach and were firing one too.

It is worth dwelling for a moment on the cold courage of tunnellers. Virtually all of them were familiar with underground work but peacetime mining dangers were objective, not cunning and ruthless like one's opponents in mine warfare. Place yourself at the face of a fighting tunnel 30m (100ft) below the surface, cramped and breathless in the dank air. Between you and the shafthead is 200m (650ft) of narrow gallery, stretching away into the Stygian gloom, its timbers bowed and creaking under pressure. Any minute, the unseen enemy might blow a camouflet and that crushing weight of earth will bear down on your torso.

William Hackett was a 42-year-old coal miner from the north of England, serving with a tunnelling company. In the small hours of 22 June 1916, Hackett and his tunnelling shift were advancing a gallery in the Givenchy sector when the Germans fired a camouflet.

The resulting collapse pinned a young Welsh clay-kicker called Thomas Williams and trapped the remainder by cutting off their retreat back to the shafthead. Eventually the Proto team broke through, anxious that their digging may trigger further collapse and alert that the Germans could fire a second charge. Three of the survivors scrambled through the narrow gap to safety but Hackett stood firm, reluctant to leave Williams. There was no time to extricate him; even Williams bid Hackett to flee. The rescuing officer then ordered Hackett clear. Still he refused: 'I am a tunneller; I must look after my mate'. Moments after the rescuers withdrew the gallery collapsed a second time, crushing Hackett and Williams. For his gallant expression of comradeship, Hackett was awarded a posthumous Victoria Cross.

Tunnellers did not always fight unseen. From time to time they blundered into one another's galleries, mounting daring raids. In his memoirs, a British tunnelling officer describes the tension of discovery: 'A cautious approach to the face. A period of listening. Deep silence. Careful work with one's hands. A short spade sparingly used. The upper part of the German timber uncovered. Our gallery is higher… another period of listening. No sound. The roof timber is lifted. A small band of earth falls with a "plop". Water. Cautiously a light is flashed, the size of the opening increased.'[10]

Once a breach had been made, fighting patrols would be thrown together armed with pistols, punch daggers, knuckle-dusters and other vicious short-range weapons. Encounters with the enemy were violent and confused. In the darkness of a tiny fighting gallery, Canadian tunnellers learnt to grab for an opponent's shoulder: if it had an epaulette, the owner was German. Lieutenant John Westacott of the 2nd Canadian Tunnelling Company describes one such skirmish:

> The Germans were taken completely by surprise. The man in front of me turned round… but he sort of hesitated. It must have been the grotesque sight of a hooded body coming at him. I shot him before he recovered from the shock, at the same time keeping my body down to allow the others behind to shoot over me. The German party never stood a chance… the fighting did not last more than perhaps two or three minutes.
> *Lieutenant John Westacott, Barrie Papers, RE Museum Library*

Experiences like this left their mark. With admirable candour for a man of his generation, Lieutenant Westacott admits that after the war he 'broke up… went to pieces' and spent three months in a dark room.

However, for the most part, work underground was mundane, back-breaking graft. Captain Grant Grieve claims that 'difficulty and danger were dismissed by veterans as unworthy of comparison with sheer weariness'.[11] Systems of work varied but a 24-hour period at the tunnel face was usually divided into eight- or six-hour shifts. A mining section would work four days in the front line, followed by four days of 'rest', which normally involved fatigue duties, for instance ferrying timber supports forwards for one of the 'resting' shifts at the front to send down the tunnels. Infantry units were often called upon to assist in these logistic tasks. One Christmas 1916 diary entry illuminates the burden on tunnelling companies: 'No work [today]. First time this has happened to this unit'.[12]

Their reward was the grim satisfaction of delivering an almighty blow. Once judged by survey to be beneath the objective, tunnellers excavated a mine chamber sufficient to house the required quantity of explosive. Most mines were 'over-charged' i.e. designed to create a crater. Tunnellers experimented with different varieties of explosive compound, eventually

---

10. Memoirs of Major F. J. Mulqueen, RE Museum Library
11. *Tunnellers*, Captain W. Grant Grieve, 1936
12. 252nd Tunnelling Company War Diary

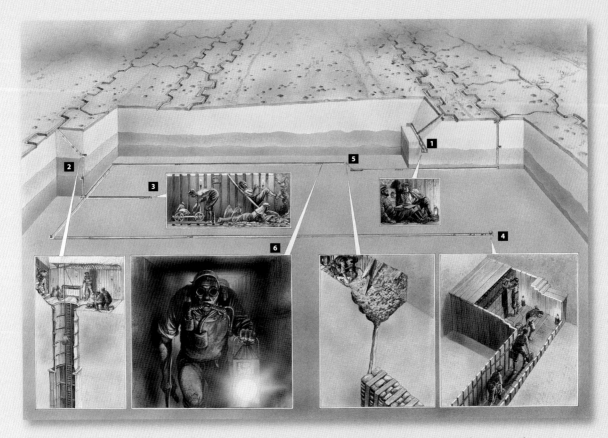

THE WAR UNDERGROUND – MINING OPERATIONS UNDER MESSINES RIDGE 1916–17 (pp. 28–29)

This cutaway scene is for illustrative purposes and so contrives events in false proximity. However, the geological layering and tunnel distances are accurate – if generic – depictions of the Messines Ridge tunnelling environment. Beneath topsoil there is the band of pale sandy clay in which shallow defensive systems were commonplace. The German listening post (1) is a good example, sitting at the end of a short lateral system accessed from their front line. Anything deeper required penetration of the saturated 'Kemmel Sands' (*Schwimmsand* to the Germans) by way of 'tubbed' shafts (2). The inset shows a British steel shaft sunk down through the sand into blue Paniselian clay. As seen here, British tunnellers favoured the security of support line shaftheads. Strange is it may seem, the clay really is that bright – though this is heightened by oxidization. Once at the required depth, a lateral allows for multiple offensive tunnels to be driven towards the German lines: redundancy was an imperative. Clay-kickers can be seen at work in the centre tunnel (3), bagging spoil for transfer to the surface via trolleys, windlass and man. The rhythmic efficiency of this technique is readily apparent. Nativity play headdress being sported by the lower 'face-man' was necessary to prevent spoil going down the back of his neck. Note the canary cage and candles: light levels have been increased for clarity. Fresh air is provided by pumping stations throughout the system (2). Paniselian clay expands on contact with oxygen, thus support

sets were spaced. This is evident throughout the illustration. Having reached German lines undetected, mine chambers (4) were loaded with explosive, either in tins or bags. All available space was utilized; narrow cavities between containers were filled with slabs of guncotton. Having set the charge, tunnellers 'tamped' back along the tunnel with sandbags to a distance at least one and a half times the depth of their charge. This ensured a skyward blast profile. Not all projects reached fruition. A successful German countermining operation has been conducted against the third project here. Careful survey by listeners using bar compasses enabled the charges to be directed accurately and their tamped torpedo camouflet (5) has entombed the British face pair, leaving the nearby trolley operator partially trapped. Carbon monoxide released by the explosion has probably already killed him. It necessitated 'Proto' breathing apparatus for rescue teams (6) who were also equipped with electric lamps for safety and portability. The scale of this Proto inset highlights how cramped and claustrophobic Great War tunnels were, a pressure compounded immeasurably by constant fear of camouflet, carbon monoxide, flooding and collapse. Tunnelling demanded extraordinary nerve but also stamina; most memoirs dwell more on fatigue than terror. This *magnum opus* for the tunnelling companies under Messines Ridge was 18 months in the making.

settling on ammonal. It was a high explosive but with a burn rate slow enough to create a good 'lift' of earth. An added bonus was its low volatility; ammonal did not detonate if struck or lit. This gave tunnellers confidence. On the flip side, it degraded rapidly when wet so ammonal charges were always placed in tins or rubber bags. Guncotton slabs were used as a primer charge. As we shall see in the case of Messines, some mines were massive – 25 tonnes and more – and would carve craters hundreds of metres wide.

Blast waves follow the path of least resistance so even in the case of small camouflets, it was essential to 'tamp' any mine charge – blocking the route you took to plant the explosive. Otherwise your own galleries would feel the force. The rule of thumb for tamping was one and a half times the distance between the mine and its objective; that way you could guarantee that it would direct itself in the direction intended. Sandbags were the best means of achieving this and tamping was another reason to make tunnels small.

Leads fed back through the tamping and made their way to the surface where, when the time came, they would be plugged into a T-bar 'exploder' of the type all will be familiar with from old B-movies involving the destruction of railway locomotives. It was the tunnelling officer's privilege to push down on the plunger at the appointed hour, and bring those weeks and months of perilous labour to spectacular fruition.

THE BRITISH

Aside from grasping the upper hand below ground, the BEF was making great conceptual strides on the surface and above it. In 1914, Britain's Royal Flying Corps deployed to France with 50 small observation planes. By summer 1917, the force had exceeded 1,000 and included the whole panoply of capabilities one would expect of a modern air force, even dedicated 'multi-role' aircraft. Strategic bombing and the establishment of a separate air service followed not long after. In terms of air-to-ground integration, the BEF were surprisingly advanced. Slow-moving machines lent themselves well to 'close air support' missions and if miniaturization had allowed for infantry to be equipped with wireless, the possibilities could have been endless. As it was, they made clever use of identification panels and klaxons to maintain contact and demarcate the battlefield.

The science of artillery had also been transformed. Firing over open sights was the norm in 1914; not two years later it was already the stuff of dire emergency. The basics of indirect fire with forward observation had been mastered by 1917 and genuinely modern techniques were nascent: 'silent' registration (combination of gun line survey and ballistic extrapolation data to fire accurately without ranging shots), flash spotting and sound ranging for counterbattery location, and complex fuzing. Protection of infantry in the assault remained the chief preoccupation and artillerymen were perfecting the 'creeping barrage' – light field gun shells laying a curtain of fire ahead of advancing units.

Creeping barrages suited deliberate, limited operations very well. But they required timetables and planned pauses; this was no way to throw off the fetters of prescriptive planning. One (albeit partial) answer arrived with the tank. First used in limited numbers on the Somme the previous September, tanks were available in ever-increasing concentrations throughout 1917 and already on their fourth iteration. The tank's primary contribution at this stage

Sapper William Hackett embodies the spirit and determination of tunnellers on both sides. After his death, comrades used their own wages to help support Hackett's wife and children, one of whom was already invalided by a coal-mining accident aged 14. (RE Museum VI.27.08)

was wire crushing. For so long the bane of all infantrymen on the Western Front, wire had hitherto precluded any semblance of tactical surprise: its destruction always warranted lengthy preparatory bombardment. Tanks also provided an armoured platform for machine guns and light artillery (naval 6-pdr) guns to provide infantry with intimate direct fire support when tackling strongpoints in depth.

However, at this stage, tanks were still defined more by their limitations than capabilities. Unreliable, slow and lacking manoeuvrability, only female (machine-gun armed) variants were capable of firing on the move with any accuracy. Target acquisition was limited to narrow slits. They were horrendous to crew: hot, noxious and lacking any kind of suspension. Most important of all, they were vulnerable. Though impervious to most small arms, armour plate would 'spall' – flakes of steel detaching from the inside and flying about the interior. Armour-piercing small arms ammunition and any artillery round would penetrate. Once hit, they were terrifyingly flammable.

Therefore, in time-honoured fashion, infantrymen were fixing most problems for themselves. Popular notions of Tommy Atkins going 'over the top' in orderly parade-ground ranks have always been a simplification; by 1917 they were already history. Modern small-unit infantry tactics owe much to February 1917's well-considered manual, *Instructions for the training of platoons in offensive action*.

Principles of 'fire and movement' were nothing new to British infantry; skirmishing riflemen in Wellington's Peninsula Army had employed simple variants. But now 36-man platoons were structured around the basic functions of suppression and assault. One nine-man section supported the platoon's Lewis light machine gun; another was equipped with 'rifle bombs' – a Mills Bomb (hand grenade) fired by a blank cartridge from a cup attachment on the end of the rifle. Having created an effective weight of fire with this half of his force, the platoon commander then assaulted the objective with his section of 'bombers'; the fourth and final section forming a reserve.

ORDERS OF BATTLE

BRITISH EXPEDITIONARY FORCE

Note: Vital as they were, space precludes detailing formation support units like Royal Flying Corps, artillery, engineers, pioneer, cavalry and logistics – less tanks and tunnelling companies. This information is readily available in the National Archive records and British Official History or by correspondence with the author.

SECOND ARMY – GEN. SIR HERBERT PLUMER

X Corps – Lt. Gen. Sir Thomas Morland

23rd Division – Maj. Gen. J. M. Babington
68th Infantry Brigade – Brig. Gen. G. N. Colville
    10th Bn. Northumberland Fusiliers
    11th Bn. Northumberland Fusiliers
    12th Bn. Durham Light Infantry
    13th Bn. Durham Light Infantry
69th Infantry Brigade – Brig. Gen. T. S. Lambert
    11th Bn. West Yorkshire Regiment
    8th Bn. Green Howards
    9th Bn. Green Howards
    10th Bn. Duke of Wellington's Regiment
70th Infantry Brigade – Brig. Gen. H. Gordon
    11th Bn. Sherwood Foresters
    8th Bn. King's Own Yorkshire Light Infantry
    8th Bn. York and Lancaster Regiment
    9th Bn. York and Lancaster Regiment

47th (2nd London) Division – Maj. Gen. Sir G. F. Gorringe
140th Infantry Brigade – Brig. Gen. H. P. B. L. Kennedy
    1/6th Bn. London Regiment (City of London Rifles)
    1/7th Bn. London Regiment (City of London)
    1/8th Bn. London Regiment (Post Office Rifles)
    1/15th Bn. London Regiment (Civil Service Rifles)
141st Infantry Brigade – Brig. Gen. R. McDougall
    1/17th Bn. London Regiment (Poplar and Stepney Rifles)
    1/18th Bn. London Regiment (London Irish Rifles)
    1/19th Bn. London Regiment (St Pancras)
    1/20th Bn. London Regiment (Blackheath and Woolwich)
142nd Infantry Brigade – Brig. Gen. V. T. Bailey
    1/21st Bn. London Regiment (1st Surrey Rifles)
    1/22nd Bn. London Regiment (The Queen's)
    1/23rd Bn. London Regiment (County of London)
    1/24th Bn. London Regiment (The Queen's)

41st (Southern and Home Counties) Division – Maj. Gen.
    S. T. B. Lawford
122nd Infantry Brigade – Brig. Gen. F. W. Towsey
    12th Bn. East Surrey Regiment
    15th Bn. Hampshire Regiment
    11th Bn. Royal West Kent Regiment
    18th Bn. King's Royal Rifle Corps

123rd Infantry Brigade – Brig. Gen. C. W. E. Gordon
    11th Bn. Queen's Regiment
    10th Bn. Royal West Kent Regiment
    23rd Bn. Middlesex Regiment
    20th Bn. Durham Light Infantry
124th Infantry Brigade – Brig. Gen. W. F. Clemson
    11th Bn. Queen's Regiment
    26th Bn. Royal Fusiliers
    32nd Bn. Royal Fusiliers
    21st Bn. King's Royal Rifle Corps

24th Division – Maj. Gen. L. J. Bols
17th Infantry Brigade – Brig. Gen. P. V. P. Stone
    8th Bn. East Kent Regiment ('Buffs')
    1st Bn. Royal Fusiliers
    12th Bn. Royal Fusiliers
    3rd Bn. Rifle Brigade
72nd Infantry Brigade – Brig. Gen. W. F. Sweny
    8th Bn. Queen's Regiment
    9th Bn. East Surrey Regiment
    8th Bn. Royal West Kent Regiment
    1st Bn. North Staffordshire Regiment
73rd Infantry Brigade – Brig. Gen. W. J. Dugan
    9th Bn. Royal Sussex Regiment
    7th Bn. Northamptonshire Regiment
    13th Bn. Middlesex Regiment
    2nd Bn. Leinster Regiment

IX Corps – Lt. Gen. Sir Alexander Hamilton-Gordon

19th (Western) Division – Maj. Gen. C. D. Shute
56th Infantry Brigade – Brig. Gen. E. Craig-Brown
    7th Bn. King's Own Regiment
    7th Bn. East Lancashire Regiment
    7th Bn. South Lancashire Regiment
    7th Bn. North Lancashire Regiment
57th Infantry Brigade – Brig. Gen. T. A. Cubitt
    10th Bn. Royal Warwickshire Regiment
    8th Bn. Gloucestershire Regiment
    10th Bn. Worcestershire Regiment
    8th Bn. North Staffordshire Regiment
58th Infantry Brigade – Brig. Gen. A. E. Glasgow
    9th Bn. Cheshire Regiment
    9th Bn. Royal Welsh Fusiliers Regiment
    9th Bn. Welsh Regiment
    6th Bn. Wiltshire Regiment

16th (Irish) Division – Maj. Gen. W. B. Hickie
47th Infantry Brigade – Brig. Gen. G. E. Pereira
    6th Bn. Royal Irish Regiment
    6th Bn. Connaught Rangers
    7th Bn. Leinster Regiment
    8th Bn. Royal Munster Fusiliers

48th Infantry Brigade – Brig. Gen. F. W. Ramsey
    7th Bn. Royal Irish Rifles
    1st Bn. Royal Munster Fusiliers
    8th Bn. Royal Dublin Fusiliers
    9th Bn. Royal Dublin Fusiliers
49th Infantry Brigade – Brig. Gen. P. Leveson-Gower
    7th Bn. Royal Inniskilling Fusiliers
    8th Bn. Royal Inniskilling Fusiliers
    7th Bn. Royal Irish Fusiliers
    8th Bn. Royal Irish Fusiliers

36th (Ulster) Division – Maj. Gen. O. S. W. Nugent
107th Infantry Brigade – Brig. Gen. W. N. Withycombe
    8th Bn. Royal Irish Rifles (East Belfast Volunteers)
    9th Bn. Royal Irish Rifles (West Belfast Volunteers)
    10th Bn. Royal Irish Rifles (South Belfast Volunteers)
    15th Bn. Royal Irish Rifles (North Belfast Volunteers)
108th Infantry Brigade – Brig. Gen. C. R. J. Griffith
    11th Bn. Royal Irish Rifles (South Antrim Volunteers)
    12th Bn. Royal Irish Rifles (Mid Antrim Volunteers)
    13th Bn. Royal Irish Rifles (1st County Down Volunteers)
    9th Bn. Royal Irish Fusiliers (Armagh, Monaghan & Cavan Volunteers)
109th Infantry Brigade – Brig. Gen. A. St. Q. Ricardo
    9th Bn. Royal Inniskilling Fusiliers (Tyrone Volunteers)
    10th Bn. Royal Inniskilling Fusiliers (Derry Volunteers)
    11th Bn. Royal Inniskilling Fusiliers (Donegal & Fermanagh Volunteers)
    14th Bn. Royal Irish Rifles (Young Citizen Volunteers of Belfast)

11th (Northern) Division – Maj. Gen. H. R. Davies
32nd Infantry Brigade – Brig. Gen. T. H. F. Price
    9th Bn. West Yorkshire Regiment
    6th Bn. Green Howards
    8th Bn. Duke of Wellington's Regiment
    6th Bn. York and Lancaster Regiment
33rd Infantry Brigade – Brig. Gen. A. C. Daly
    6th Bn. Lincolnshire Regiment
    6th Bn. Border Regiment
    7th Bn. South Staffordshire Regiment
    9th Bn. Sherwood Foresters
34th Infantry Brigade – Brig. Gen. S. H. Pedley
    8th Bn. Northumberland Fusiliers
    9th Bn. Lancashire Fusiliers
    5th Bn. Dorset Regiment
    11th Bn. Manchester Regiment

II ANZAC Corps – Lt. Gen. Sir Alexander Godley
25th (North Western) Division – Maj. Gen. E. G. T. Bainbridge
7th Infantry Brigade – Brig. Gen. C. C. Onslow
    10th Bn. Cheshire Regiment

    3rd Bn. Worcestershire Regiment
    8th Bn. North Lancashire Regiment
    1st Bn. Wiltshire Regiment
74th Infantry Brigade – Brig. Gen. H. K. Bethell
    11th Bn. Lancashire Fusiliers
    13th Bn. Cheshire Regiment
    9th Bn. North Lancashire Regiment
    2nd Bn. Royal Irish Rifles
75th Infantry Brigade – Brig. Gen. H. B. D. Baird
    11th Bn. Cheshire Regiment
    8th Bn. Border Regiment
    2nd Bn. South Lancashire Regiment
    8th Bn. South Lancashire Regiment

New Zealand Division – Maj. Gen. Sir Andrew Russell
1st New Zealand Brigade – Brig. Gen. E. H. B. Brown
    1st Bn. Auckland Regiment
    1st Bn. Canterbury Regiment
    1st Bn. Otago Regiment
    1st Bn. Wellington Regiment
2nd New Zealand Brigade – Brig. Gen. W. G. Braithwaite
    2nd Bn. Auckland Regiment
    2nd Bn. Canterbury Regiment
    2nd Bn. Otago Regiment
    2nd Bn. Wellington Regiment
3rd New Zealand Brigade – Brig. Gen. H. T. Fulton
    1st New Zealand Rifle Bn.
    2nd New Zealand Rifle Bn.
    3rd New Zealand Rifle Bn.
    4th New Zealand Rifle Bn.

3rd Australian Division – Maj. Gen. John Monash
9th Australian Brigade – Brig. Gen. A. Jobson
    33rd Bn. (New South Wales)
    34th Bn. (New South Wales)
    35th Bn. (New South Wales)
    36th Bn. (New South Wales)
10th Australian Brigade – Brig. Gen. W. R. McNicoll
    37th Bn. (Victoria)
    38th Bn. (Victoria)
    39th Bn. (Victoria)
    40th Bn. (Victoria)
11th Australian Brigade – Brig. Gen. A. Cannan
    41st Bn. (Outer States)
    42nd Bn. (Outer States)
    43rd Bn. (Outer States)
    44th Bn. (Outer States)

4th Australian Division – Maj. Gen. William Holmes
4th Australian Brigade – Brig. Gen. C. H. Brand
    13th Bn. (New South Wales)
    14th Bn. (Victoria)

15th Bn. (Queensland and Tasmania)

16th Bn. (South and Western Australia)

12th Australian Brigade – Brig. Gen. J. C. Robertson

    45th Bn. (New South Wales)

    46th Bn. (Victoria)

    47th Bn. (Queensland and Tasmania)

    48th Bn. (South and Western Australia)

13th Australian Brigade – Brig. Gen. T. W. Glasgow

    49th Bn. (Queensland)

    50th Bn. (South Australia)

    51st Bn. (Western Australia)

    52nd Bn. (South and Western Australia & Tasmania)

Heavy Branch, Machine Gun Corps elements:

II Tank Brigade – Col. A. Courage

    A Bn.

    B Bn.

Royal Engineers Tunnelling Companies involved in the Messines
    mining offensive at various stages (* denotes present on
    7 June):

1st Australian Tunnelling Company*

2nd Australian Tunnelling Company

1st Canadian Tunnelling Company*

2nd Canadian Tunnelling Company

3rd Canadian Tunnelling Company*

171st Tunnelling Company*

172nd Tunnelling Company

175th Tunnelling Company

250th Tunnelling Company*

GERMAN
FOURTH ARMY – GEN. DER INFANTERIE SIXT VON ARMIN
XIX Corps – Gruppe Wytschaete – Gen. der Kavallerie von Laffert

204th (Württemberg) Infantry Division – Gen.Lt. von Stein

    413th Infantry Regiment

    120th Reserve Infantry Regiment

    414th Infantry Regiment

35th (Prussian) Infantry Division – Gen.Lt. von Hahn

    176th Infantry Regiment

    141st Infantry Regiment

    61st Infantry Regiment

2nd (East Prussian) Infantry Division – Gen.Lt. Reiser

    44th Infantry Regiment

    33rd Fusilier Regiment

    4th Grenadier Regiment

40th (Saxon) Infantry Division – Gen.Lt. Meister

    104th Infantry Regiment

    134th Infantry Regiment

    181st Infantry Regiment

3rd (Bavarian) Infantry Division – Gen. der Infanterie von
    Wenninger

    23rd Bavarian Infantry Regiment

    18th Bavarian Infantry Regiment

    17th Bavarian Infantry Regiment

Counterattack [*Eingreif*] Divisions in Gruppe Wytschaete Sector:

7th Infantry Division – Gen.Lt. von der Eich

    26th Infantry Regiment

    163rd Infantry Regiment

    393rd Infantry Regiment

1st Guards Reserve Infantry Division – Gen.Lt. von Tiede

    1st Guards Reserve Infantry Regiment

    2nd Guards Reserve Infantry Regiment

    64th Reserve Infantry Regiment

German flanking formations involved in the battle 7 June:

From Gruppe Ypern to north:

119th Infantry Division – Gen.Lt. Grünert

From Gruppe Lille to South:

4th (Bavarian) Infantry Division – Gen.Lt. Prinz Franz von Bayern

    5th Bavarian Infantry Regiment

    9th Bavarian Infantry Regiment

    5th Bavarian Reserve Infantry Regiment

Other relieving Divisions brought in by Fourth Army after
    7 June, whole or in part:

11th (Silesian) Infantry Division

16th (Bavarian) Infantry Division

22nd Reserve Infantry Division

23rd (Saxon) Reserve Infantry Division

24th (Saxon) Infantry Division

195th Infantry Division

207th Infantry Division

OPPOSING PLANS

THE GERMANS

General von Armin's Fourth Army understood the significance of Messines Ridge. To the Germans it was *Wijtschatebogen* – Wytschaete Salient. Intelligence updates emanating from HQ Army Group North (the equivalent of BEF's GHQ) were warning of potential attack throughout the early months of 1917. There was little that could be done to improve physical defences on the ridge; it lay beyond the area affected by Germany's withdrawal to the bespoke Siegfried Stellung. However, the latest defensive doctrine was applied, leading to a marked shift in emphasis from previous years.

Awakened to the costliness of defending front lines with swollen garrisons, German planners came to accept a degree of penetration by assaulting enemy forces and instead built their doctrine around counterattack. *Eingreifentaktik* – literally 'intervention tactic' – was in essence defence in depth. Consequently, historians have also used terms like 'flexible' and 'elastic' defence.

As broached in the previous chapter, the key realization was that infantrymen were not the vital component to physical defence: wire, artillery and machine-gun fire could achieve that. Thus, they dispensed with a strong linear front line and created a *Vorwärtszone* – 'outpost zone', a chequerboard of mutually supporting strongpoints known as *Widerstandsnester*. In effect this drew the enemy in, throwing him off balance for the moment when he hit the *Widerstand* itself – 'resistance line'. This resembled more conventional revetted trench systems in concentric lines a few hundred metres apart, protected by thick bands of wire often configured to draw attackers into pre-selected 'killing areas'. Ideally, the *Widerstand* was situated on a reverse slope to maximize the ambush.

Passive as all this sounds, it was merely creating the conditions for counterattack by dedicated units – *Eingreif* divisions – held beyond the battle zone (and therefore protected from enemy artillery) until the decisive moment when an enemy force had overextended itself.

Yet *Eingreifentaktik* is sometimes misapprehended. The point behind *Eingreif* formations was to prevent enemy penetration beyond the battle zone. Though rehearsed in their roles, plans and timetables were not concrete. Planners were looking for a specific effect known as *Gegenstoss* (counterstroke), more akin to moving a chess piece than swinging a punch. Eingreif units did not necessarily counterattack; they might simply reinforce existing defences at a decisive point.

Aside from making do with legacy defences, on Messines Ridge the theory was disrupted by the fact that its vital crest lay in the forward area. Spanbroekmolen knoll – the cornerstone of their centre – sat in the outpost zone. Consequently, Gruppe Wytschaete's defence of Messines Ridge was a hybrid affair, especially at the tactical level. The map on p. 48 denotes the principal trench systems that backed up Messines Ridge. The curved front was protected by an intermediate supplementary position that resembled the string of a bow. This was the Sehnen Stellung, hereafter referred to by its British name as the Oosttaverne Line.

Gruppe Wytschaete had four divisions occupying the ridge; the southern extremity fell within the purview of Gruppe Lille's 4th (Bavarian) Infantry Division. In the north around Hill 60 was the 204th Infantry Division from Württemberg, brought in as a reaction to the intelligence assessments of impending attack. The shoulder of Messines Ridge was held by the Prussians of the 35th Infantry Division, its midriff by their compatriots in the 2nd Infantry Division. At the lower end around the village of Messines were Saxons from 40th Infantry Division.

Each division had three regiments in the line, disposed side by side. This gave each one a slice of front, much the most efficient way of managing duty cycles. One battalion was kept at the fore, manning outposts and front-line trench systems. The second occupied the support trenches one kilometre back and the third was held in reserve, in this case at the Oosttaverne Line. Although each battalion sector had a headquarters, primacy was afforded to the *Kampftruppenkommandeur* (KTK) – commander of forward troops. Under the ethos previously explained, the KTK was going to be in the best position to read the battle, apportion local reinforcements from the reserve line and prioritize artillery fire. It was an onerous responsibility for men often just holding the rank of *Hauptmann* (Captain).

As it became increasingly apparent that the British had designs on Messines Ridge, General von Kuhl, Army Group North's Chief of Staff, expressed concern about the vulnerability of Gruppe Wytschaete's dispositions. He mooted a plan to Army Group Commander Kronprinz Rupprecht for withdrawal to the Oosttaverne Line. It seems a notion at odds with the value of Messines Ridge until one considers that clinging so stubbornly to a topographical feature was also contradictory to strategic and doctrinal fashion.

In any event, Gruppe Wytschaete's commander, General von Laffert, lobbied hard to remain on the ridge. He reasoned (correctly) that the crest

LEFT
German defensive doctrine demanded an aggressive spirit from all force elements, not solely dedicated counterattack formations. Moreover, the emphasis was on making a timely and decisive contribution to defence: these troops are lying in wait for whoever blunders over that bank. (IWM Q 45583)

RIGHT
General von Laffert believed that his artillery would assist Gruppe Wytschaete in holding the crest of Messines Ridge for up to 12 hours. Fearsome-looking weapons like this 21cm heavy mortar (in essence a short-range howitzer) encouraged that impression but of course it's all relative; Plumer had more. (IWM Q 23783)

Kuhl planned to vacate overlooked the Oosttaverne Line. A better option would be the Warneton Line – one of four Army-level reserve trench systems east of the Ypres Salient – but that would necessitate retirements elsewhere, so better all round to stay put. Backed by his subordinates and a confident artillery commander, Laffert had faith in his ability to hold the crest for at least 12 hours, time enough for the two *Eingreif* divisions behind him to tip the balance in Germany's favour.

A major part of Kuhl's rationale was that withdrawal would also stymie Britain's mining offensive. If they had known what lay beneath their feet, there would have been no argument. But they did not. German countermining efforts – a campaign called *Quetschungen*, 'crushing operations' – had abated in the belief that British mining activity was diminished. They were right inasmuch as no blows had been delivered for months; what they failed to consider was the possibility that a coordinated offensive lay dormant.

Oberstleutnant Otto von Füsslein, mining commander for Fourth Army, had assumed responsibility for *Quetschungen* in September 1916 – after British offensive preparations were well under way. Until May 1917, the area south of river Douve (where the British had eight mining projects) was not his bailiwick. Nonetheless, he was making confident assertions based on limited successes and sketchy information. On 30 April, he opined at an Army Group North conference that the threat was deemed to be 'nicht mehr möglich' – no longer possible. By 10 May, he had admitted that a number of deep mines 'may have been prepared' and 'should there be an attack, it may be preceded by large explosions at some... places', yet two weeks later he briefed favourably to Laffert that the danger from mine explosions was not great. Perhaps most tellingly, from 12 May the mine threat paragraph was removed from Fourth Army's weekly situation reports.

THE BRITISH

Earthquaking the ridge
Years later, tunnellers talked of Messines Ridge with great reverence and unconcealed pride. In his unofficial history of British tunnelling, Captain Grant Grieve gushes that 'never in the history of warfare has the miner played such vital part in a battle'.[13] On its tenth anniversary, an anonymous tunneller proffered that there are still those 'who feel a thrill as they remember [Messines]; who heave a sigh and perchance raise a glass in memory of brave days that were'.[14] It is unsurprising: the BEF's tunnelling companies toiled for nearly two years in preparation for Messines – surely their crowning achievement of the entire war. Things took on a different character after that; the heyday of mining passed.

As has been touched upon, this mining offensive germinated from a 12 May 1915 diary entry by Norton-Griffiths: 'An examination of trench maps... leads to the belief that if mining efforts were concentrated in front of Wytschaete... a good and perhaps most useful mining programme might materially help to straighten out our line. It should be possible for mines to break the line at say 6 given points.'[15]

13. *Tunnellers*, Captain Grant Grieve, 1936
14. 'Messines', 'Tunneller' (Anon), *RE Journal*, 1937
15. War Diary, Major Sir John Norton-Griffiths, National Archive

It is no coincidence that the date of that diary entry comes just one week after 170th Tunnelling Company first penetrated Kemmel Sand successfully – the prerequisite to deep mining. His scheme achieved approval on 6 January 1916, burgeoning under the patronage of BEF's Engineer-in-Chief, Brigadier-General Fowke, and of course Plumer. Norton-Griffiths parted company with his beloved Moles in March 1916, destined (as befits such a romantic figure) for a mission denying the Germans the oilfields and grain reserves of Romania. Colonel Harvey took up the reins and saw Messines through. It is curious that so secret an operation never carried a codename; nor did many of the constituent individual projects. By contrast, the German *Pioniere* subdivided their front into codenamed sectors, all bearing girls' names: Erica, Christine, Frieda, etc.

Most accounts state that the scheme grew from six to 25 mines. However, the most authoritative research now concludes that there were up to 49 proposed avenues of attack; certainly, the figure of 25 only describes mines either blown or lost – not those that would have been undertaken had time and geology permitted. The schematic on p. 44 outlines the undertaking and summarizes a few vital statistics for each charge. At one time or another there were nine tunnelling companies active under Messines Ridge (see Order of battle).

Hill 60 marks the northern extremity of the Messines offensive. In mining terms, the area beyond was unsuitable due to a complete stalemate: it was a warren of defensive systems above thick belts of Kemmel Sand. Both Hill 60 and its neighbouring bump 'The Caterpillar' were man-made spoil heaps, relics of the Ypres–Comines railway cutting construction. The area enjoyed a reputation for damp (acetylene lamps were adopted there because candles did not stay alight) and difficult ground. Hitherto, all workings had been conducted at only 5m (16ft). In summer 1915, 175th Tunnelling Company arrived determined to get deep. By starting 200m (650ft) behind the front lines, they drove a long timbered incline down to firm blue clay 28m (92ft) below the surface. From here the Moles started an offensive gallery that attracted the epithet 'Berlin Tunnel' – infantry work parties extracted so much wet mud from it, they were convinced Germany must be the destination.

After a reshuffle, the next tenants at Hill 60 were the Canadians. They put a fork in the Berlin Tunnel and burrowed beneath both Hill 60 and The Caterpillar in August 1916. Encountering wet and unstable ground short of the objective on Hill 60, they cut their losses and constructed a twin mine chamber packed with 24,300kg (53,500lb) of ammonal. The Caterpillar thwarted their plans too and they were forced to branch right, though here they overcame the deviation by planting a 32,750kg (71,000lb) monster.

By now the incline was under real pressure, requiring eight pumps to prevent flooding. The mine charges were in watertight cans with three times the normal number of detonators but the principal danger was to men maintaining the tunnels and manning defensive works – a well-placed German camouflet would fill the Berlin Tunnel with quicksand. A new vertical shaft was started and, in November 1916, the Australians arrived to continue it. Using a network of dummy picks banging away at dead-end shallower projects, the Australians aimed to keep the *Pioniere* off the scent. A German tunnelling officer captured during a raid betrayed the presence of a deep countermine, which was then blown with a large camouflet.

The Australians completed their shaft safely, sealing off the frail incline, but the game of cat and mouse continued beneath Hill 60 right up until

The waterlogged geology of Flanders posed a perennial challenge to tunnellers. Pumps like these were often operated around the clock – not the most varied of labours. Note the trucks and spoil windlasses in the background. (IWM E 1396)

7 June 1917. *Pioniere* attacked a new protective system being built by the Australians that March. Whilst awaiting rescue, an entombed listener had the extraordinary aplomb to continue his shift, ascertaining the presence of a new deep countermine nearby. Experts deduced that German digging rates would only bring them onto the two charges if they knew exactly where they were going. This being unlikely, all activity ceased in that area and the tunnellers held their breath.

Next was the Canadian project at St Eloi. The scene of much tactical mining activity throughout spring 1916, the deep shaft (named 'Queen Victoria') was not started until August. Relatively speaking, St Eloi was a straightforward venture because German countermining concentrated on other areas. Security was assisted by survey of a devious route to the target area. But the clay was particularly hard going and it is typical of histories like this to skim over the months of graft simply because they lack anecdotal colour. It took ten months to dig 500m (1,600ft). At the end of it, the Canadians planted 43,450kg (95,600lb) of explosives – the largest single charge in the history of military mining.

Conversely, the Germans always knew something was up at Hollandscheschuur. Canadians here had made rapid progress, exploiting 100m (330ft) beyond the German front line by March 1916 but German observers spotted the shafthead entrance and shelled it liberally, scoring a brace of direct hits. They then followed this up with two speculative but heavy camouflets in May and June. It called for patience from the Canadians. By keeping quiet for a month, the Germans deduced that the blows had been a success and moved on. Subsequently, three charges were laid with utmost stealth in July 1916.

With so much excavation occurring on the Ypres Salient, many might speculate why mechanical digging devices were not utilized. In the context of mine warfare, the obvious retort is the noise they would make. However, at Petit Bois, the tunnel shaft ran from 500m (1,600ft) behind the front

line. This was the perfect opportunity to trial the efficacy of a specially commissioned 'Great Shield' Stanley Heading Machine, powered by compressed air. Arriving at the front in March 1916, the seven-ton contraption was lowered tentatively down to a depth of 30m (100ft), where the offensive gallery had recently been started.

Accompanied by a team of experts, the 'Great Shield' carried the hopes of many a back-sore clay-kicker. In its first shift, it cut for eight hours at a rate of 60cm (2ft) per hour. Alas, a false dawn. Not only did it have a tendency to dive, but, as soon as the machine rested, encroaching clay set it fast. Men who might otherwise have been advancing the tunnel, sweated instead to dig out the 'Great Shield' – a false economy. Having witnessed civilian innovators failing publicly with their martial gadgets, I can picture a crestfallen retreat up the shaft ladder – cynical Moles looking on with scant sympathy. Captain Grieve's *schadenfreude* is barely concealed: 'the experts left in high dudgeon… [The machine] remains covered in shame and 80 odd feet of Flanders soil, so that no mortal eye may gaze on its abysmal failure.'[16]

Another mechanical intervention was later planned for an area known as 'The Bluff' between Hill 60 and St Eloi. Examination of the map on p. 44 will betray an alarming gap in the coverage of mine blasts at the northern end of Plumer's attack frontage. Five blows were intended, specifically to bracket a strongpoint at White Chateau. Time and resources precluded the venture unless the main gallery could be driven mechanically. Here too the machine – a Whitaker – seized. Infantry were to rue its malfunction. Fighting at White Chateau proved bitter.

Back at Petit Bois, the Moles of 250th Tunnelling Company kicked on at a determined rate of up to 50m (160ft) per week. Geology applied the brakes first; expanding clay crushed the supports, forcing them to re-timber with spaced sets. Then the Germans caused disaster. The main gallery was now beyond German lines and forming a Y-junction to make its attacks. At half six in the morning on 10 June 1916, *Pioniere* blew two overcharged mines above them. Tunnellers recall that they were speculative camouflets but the charges cratered and German infantry incorporated them into the front line. The provenance made no difference below ground: 80m (260ft) of gallery collapsed, trapping the entire 12-man shift at the face.

Rescuers toiled with frenzy to re-open the gallery but what hope of survivors? It took six and a half days to break through; if oxygen had not

16. *Tunnellers*, Captain Grant Grieve, 1936

expired, water would have. Worst fears were realized as they encountered body after body along the gallery. At length, they reached the face and there, miraculously, emerged Sapper Bedson with the glorious understatement: 'It's been a long shift. For God's sake give me a drink!' As an experienced miner, Bedson knew to crawl towards the highest point and not waste air trying to dig an exit. His comrades had disagreed and, one by one, suffocated. After a brief convalescence, Bedson applied to return to Petit Bois but his officers felt he had done enough and found a job for him in a tunnelling depot. Petit Bois was repaired, the two branches pushed out and charges placed at the end of July and mid-August 1916. *Pioniere* continued to probe but gave up once evidence of British work evaporated.

250th Tunnelling Company were a tenacious organization and undertook two geologically challenging projects further south: at Maedelstede and Peckham farms. The former warranted a parallel 'auxiliary' offensive gallery owing to threat of collapse from 'heavy ground' – clay that expanded faster than normal. Problems were compounded by the commensurate increase in spoil: at Maedelstede a covered tramway was constructed on the surface to deal with the volume being extracted. Each night it was spread out and camouflaged in rear areas. *Pioniere* remained suspicious enough to blow camouflets but in recognition of Teutonic routine, the threat to life was mitigated by withdrawing tunnellers between 1300 and 1700hrs – the only time Germans blew in this sector.

Peckham avoided any attention from *Pioniere*; perhaps they knew that geology was doing their work for them. The clay crushed timbers and buckled trolley rails. After the first charge was laid, a branch tunnel pushed left into an unforeseen seam of sand and water. Damming it off, they pushed right instead, managing to place a small 9,100kg (20,000lb) mine in waterlogged ground that soon flooded the entire network, filling it with sand and slime. The main gallery collapsed in the deluge, cutting off both mines. Imagine the exasperation as it dawned on them they needed to redig 300m (1,000ft) of parallel gallery in order to reach the main charge. It is testament to their survey skills that this was achieved with near total accuracy in March 1917. The lesser charge was beyond help.

Frictions conspired to limit the Maedelstede project as well. Abandoning their northern branch, the tunnellers concentrated on reaching a single objective with one powerful mine. Even then, it was a close-run thing. Maedelstede was one of the last-minute projects, tamped and primed on 6 June 1917.

The German strongpoint at Spanbroekmolen knoll justified a similarly massive explosion but so obvious an objective attracted countermining. Started by the indefatigable 250th Tunnelling Company in December 1915, Spanbroekmolen was a collective effort that saw both Canadian and British tunnellers in its galleries. The main charge was completed in June 1916, undetected on account of its depth. However, by early 1917, *Pioniere* had established deep workings and heard Spanbroekmolen's branch drive. Jarred by heavy camouflets, the Moles withdrew only to have their main tunnel collapsed by another that March. As with Peckham, it necessitated a complete re-excavation, the charge primed again with just hours to spare.

Mining in this central sector was capped off with a nest of four medium-sized charges at Kruisstraat, all connected to a single shaft. Relatively unmolested, the Moles were able to burrow all the way to the German forward reserve line – a distance of 700m (2,300ft).

Out of 2,226 BEF guns at Messines, Second Army had only three of these 15in. howitzers but their contribution was disproportionately great, especially in tasks such as the devastation of Messines and Wytschaete. Each shell weighed 636kg (1,400lb). (IWM Q 11661)

South of Kruisstraat the geology of Messines Ridge shifts slightly. The firm blue clay is overlaid not by a dual band of workable sandy clay and fluid Kemmel Sand but a homogeneous 30m (100ft) stratum of very wet alluvial sands – the ancient floodplain of the river Douve. This made shaft construction even more complicated as the alluvials behaved similarly to Kemmel and ran deeper. At both Ontario and Petite Douve farms, steel tubbing was required all the way down to the clay. Water and quicksand permeated nonetheless. Ontario's gallery had to divert around alluvials encountered at depth; Petite Douve's gallery employed drainage sumps at regular intervals. Working conditions were miserable.

Success was made at Ontario, though only just in time for Plumer's offensive. Petite Douve was ill fated. They completed the charge but encountered German workings on a subsequent branch gallery. 'So small was the partition of clay separating us from the enemy that he could be heard plainly talking and laughing'.[17] A camouflet left there in ambush was blown in August 1916 when the *Pioniere* trespassed. Rather than deterring them, it provoked a nasty response some days later, killing four Moles on a repair detail. Damage was too great to rectify with the Germans so close. Petite Douve earned the dubious honour of being the only mine project lost to enemy action. But the Moles won a consolation prize. Once forsaken, the galleries flooded. It soon became apparent that this water percolated into German tunnels. Thus water was diverted continually into Petite Douve to keep *Pioniere* busy at their pumps.

North-east of Ploegsteert Wood ('Plugstreet' to British soldiers) the tunnelling companies planned eight mines tucked into the base of the Messines Ridge Salient. Half of them were clustered together in an area known as Birdcage. They sunk three shafts at Birdcage in January 1916 and made good progress towards German lines to establish four charges. Once it became apparent that this eastern extremity sat outside Plumer's attack frontage, the mines were abandoned.

17. *Tunnellers*, Captain Grant Grieve, 1936

Messines mines schematic and overall scheme for the Flanders offensive

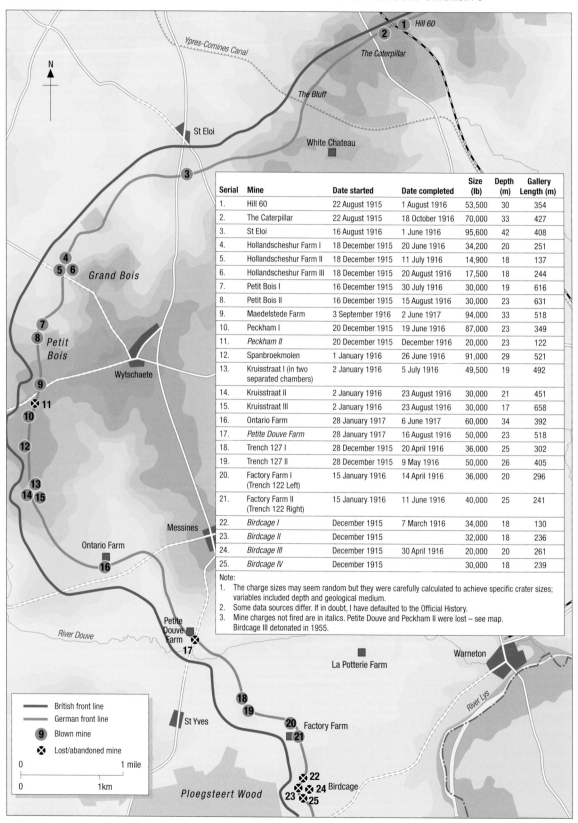

Serial	Mine	Date started	Date completed	Size (lb)	Depth (m)	Gallery Length (m)
1.	Hill 60	22 August 1915	1 August 1916	53,500	30	354
2.	The Caterpillar	22 August 1915	18 October 1916	70,000	33	427
3.	St Eloi	16 August 1916	1 June 1916	95,600	42	408
4.	Hollandscheshur Farm I	18 December 1915	20 June 1916	34,200	20	251
5.	Hollandscheshur Farm II	18 December 1915	11 July 1916	14,900	18	137
6.	Hollandscheshur Farm III	18 December 1915	20 August 1916	17,500	18	244
7.	Petit Bois I	16 December 1915	30 July 1916	30,000	19	616
8.	Petit Bois II	16 December 1915	15 August 1916	30,000	23	631
9.	Maedelstede Farm	3 September 1916	2 June 1917	94,000	33	518
10.	Peckham I	20 December 1915	19 June 1916	87,000	23	349
11.	*Peckham II*	20 December 1915	December 1916	20,000	23	122
12.	Spanbroekmolen	1 January 1916	26 June 1916	91,000	29	521
13.	Kruisstraat I (in two separated chambers)	2 January 1916	5 July 1916	49,500	19	492
14.	Kruisstraat II	2 January 1916	23 August 1916	30,000	21	451
15.	Kruisstraat III	2 January 1916	23 August 1916	30,000	17	658
16.	Ontario Farm	28 January 1917	6 June 1917	60,000	34	392
17.	*Petite Douve Farm*	28 January 1917	16 August 1916	50,000	23	518
18.	Trench 127 I	28 December 1915	20 April 1916	36,000	25	302
19.	Trench 127 II	28 December 1915	9 May 1916	50,000	26	405
20.	Factory Farm I (Trench 122 Left)	15 January 1916	14 April 1916	36,000	20	296
21.	Factory Farm II (Trench 122 Right)	15 January 1916	11 June 1916	40,000	25	241
22.	*Birdcage I*	December 1915	7 March 1916	34,000	18	130
23.	*Birdcage II*	December 1915		32,000	18	236
24.	*Birdcage III*	December 1915	30 April 1916	20,000	20	261
25.	*Birdcage IV*	December 1915		30,000	18	239

Note:
1. The charge sizes may seem random but they were carefully calculated to achieve specific crater sizes; variables included depth and geological medium.
2. Some data sources differ. If in doubt, I have defaulted to the Official History.
3. Mine charges not fired are in italics. Petite Douve and Peckham II were lost – see map. Birdcage III detonated in 1955.

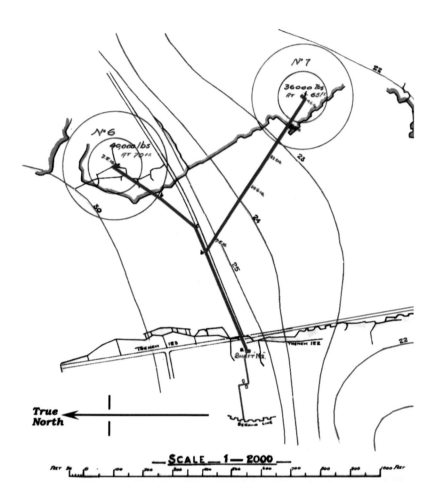

True North

SCALE 1 — 2000

The other four mines – two at Factory Farm (also sometimes termed Trench 122) and two near Trench 127 – benefited from a slightly incongruous boundary between Gruppen Wytschaete and Lille up on Messines Ridge. Consequently, Fourth Army *Pioniere*, attuned to the threat and operating environment of the Ypres Salient, had no access to this sector. Progress by 171st Tunnelling Company was correspondingly businesslike; one shift at Factory Farm clocked 10m (30ft). Alluvials played their hand, forcing a dam and branch manoeuvre at Trench 127, but all charges were tamped and primed by June 1916. Captain Hudspeth recalls toasting their health: 'We drank champagne in the [mine] chambers just before we closed them up. We four section commanders used to get through four bottles.'[18]

Tunnellers were well disposed to drink; hardly surprising in light of the stresses. Junior ranks received a double rum ration when coming off shift but drank more off duty; drunkenness was the only significant disciplinary issue that affected tunnelling companies. In his memoirs Major Dixon describes one of the parties they enjoyed when given a break from troglodyte travails: 'The dinner went well… and I can remember being so rude as to interrupt a conversation with Major Morgan in order to rush to the window as though it were the side of a ship.'[19]

18. Captain H. M. Hudspeth, Barrie Papers, RE Museum
19. *The Lighter Side of a Tunneller's Life*, Maj. H. R. Dixon, 1932 (RE Museum)

Three of the naval squadrons at Messines were equipped with Sopwith Triplanes, capable fighters with an exceptional rate of climb that pilots nicknamed the 'Tripe'. It never entered service with the RFC (as the infamous Camel arrived soon after). However, it was this aircraft that initiated Germany's fascination with triplanes. (IWM Q 66794)

As is evident from the narrative, most of the Messines mine charges lay dormant for many months. This meant long periods of tedious maintenance and a borderline neurosis that they would not detonate as planned. Leads were checked for their integrity constantly. Like a surprise party arranged too far in advance, there was always the niggling concern that something was going to upset the scheme.

Plumer's preparations

Having played second fiddle for so long, Plumer was finally being given his chance. He returned from 7 May's conference with Haig in fine spirits. Unaccustomed to being the centre of attention, Second Army HQ felt gluttonous in receipt of limitless resources. The Chief of Staff was a man with whom Plumer had developed a memorable partnership: Major-General Charles Harington. Well liked, Harington had 'an extreme simplicity of manner [and]… a memory like a card index system'.[20]

An operation of this nature was their *métier*; plans were already at an advanced stage. In keeping with the Macmullen Memorandum, Messines Ridge was a limited objective. Second Army would consolidate just east of the Oosttaverne Line. The ground in between was segmented by coloured lines, the most important of which being 'Black' – the crest of the ridge. This marked the culmination of phase one, whereupon fresh divisions would leapfrog onto the Oosttaverne Line after a pause for artillery replenishment.

As outlined previously, Plumer dedicated three corps to the attack – X, IX and II ANZAC – keeping XIV in reserve. By assaulting the perimeter of a salient, Plumer's forces were advancing on three converging axes. Thus he employed two divisions per corps in the first wave and just their third for the final push.

Plumer understood *Eingreifentaktik*: the latest edition of *German Instructions for the Defensive Battle* had been captured at Arras. In one sense, Plumer was planning an ambush of his own: capture the Oosttaverne Line with speed and momentum, then consolidate to smash German

20. *Realities of War*, Phillip Gibbs, 1920

counterattacks. Mines were intended to give his men a decisive advantage in the crucial first minutes, what American planners of the 2003 Iraq invasion called 'shock and awe'. But Gruppe Wytschaete's concentric defences had depth and counterattack would be fluid. This called for artillery, the anchor for all of Plumer's planning above ground.

Second Army's organic artillery holdings were extensively reinforced: 50 per cent of Fifth Army's heavy guns, 30 per cent of both First and Third Army's heavy guns plus an extra 34 Field Artillery Brigades on top of the 30 already integral to Plumer's infantry divisions. The table below charts comparison with Gruppe Wytschaete. Already it is evident that Laffert's confidence in his guns was probably misplaced.

Serial	British weapon type	Total	German equivalent at Messines	Total
	18-pdr	1,158	7.7cm gun	236
	4.5in. howitzer	352	10.5cm howitzer	108
	60-pdr	186	10–12cm guns	54
	6in. gun	20	15cm gun	24
	6in. howitzer	316	5.9in. howitzer	174
	8in. howitzer	108	N/A	Nil
	9.2in. gun	2	21cm gun	2
	9.2in. howitzer	108	18.5cm howitzer	40
	12in. howitzer	12	N/A	Nil
	12in. gun	1	24cm gun	2
	12in. Howitzer	3	N/A	Nil
	Totals	2,266		640

Notes:
The difference between a 'gun' and a 'howitzer' is that the latter is designed for high-angle shooting. By 1917, the distinction was becoming less relevant as all gun designs started to account for greater elevation.
These figures do not include trench mortars – Plumer had 438 medium and heavy weapons at his disposal.

There were five facets to Plumer's 'fire-plan' and it incorporated all of the techniques perfected at Arras. First was bombardment designed to destroy strongpoints, including farms and villages that the Germans had fortified. This was matched by a concerted counterbattery programme to silence their guns. These two elements involved all of the heavy guns, parcelled into detachments: 28 for physical destruction, 12 for counterbattery work. Light guns and trench mortars took on the remaining three tasks: cutting wire (for which the 18-pdrs were issued with the brand-new 106 'graze' fuze), harassment of rear areas in order to exhaust the garrison, and finally, creeping barrage for the assault itself. Harassing fire was assisted by machine-gun barrage – used effectively on Vimy Ridge that April. All but the creeping barrage formed the preparatory bombardment, due to commence (formally) on 21 May.

One problem facing the gunners was target acquisition; they could not see beyond the ridge. Here the 300 machines of II Brigade Royal Flying Corps (RFC) provided the answer. Observation was their most telling contribution at Messines Ridge. Not only did they relay corrections but photographed German trenches daily and enemy battery locations every other day. This permitted accurate battle damage assessment and hence more efficient use of resources. Throughout the preparatory bombardment, night and day bomber units would act as 'air artillery', hitting enemy aerodromes, railheads and

Messines operational objectives

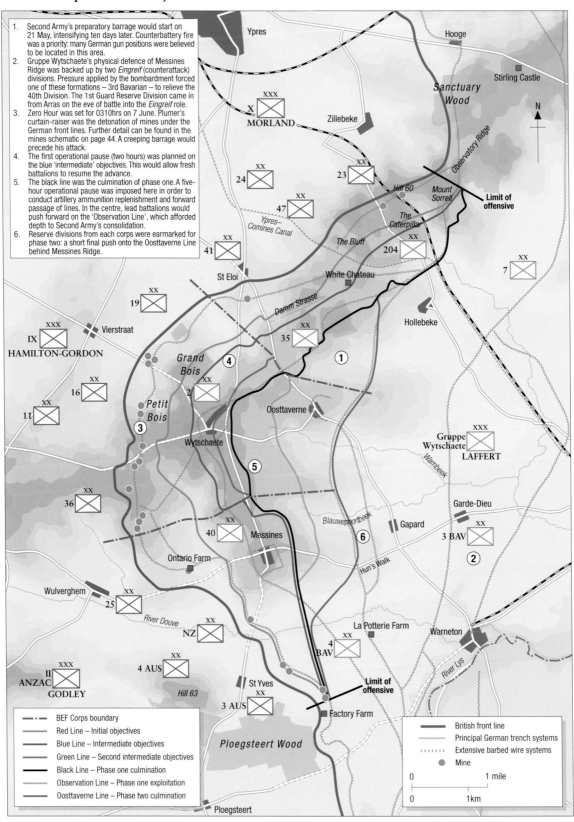

1. Second Army's preparatory barrage would start on 21 May, intensifying ten days later. Counterbattery fire was a priority: many German gun positions were believed to be located in this area.
2. Gruppe Wytschaete's physical defence of Messines Ridge was backed up by two *Eingreif* (counterattack) divisions. Pressure applied by the bombardment forced one of these formations – 3rd Bavarian – to relieve the 40th Division. The 1st Guard Reserve Division came in from Arras on the eve of battle into the *Eingreif* role.
3. Zero Hour was set for 0310hrs on 7 June. Plumer's curtain-raiser was the detonation of mines under the German front lines. Further detail can be found in the mines schematic on page 44. A creeping barrage would precede his attack.
4. The first operational pause (two hours) was planned on the blue 'intermediate' objectives. This would allow fresh battalions to resume the advance.
5. The black line was the culmination of phase one. A five-hour operational pause was imposed here in order to conduct artillery ammunition replenishment and forward passage of lines. In the centre, lead battalions would push forward on the 'Observation Line', which afforded depth to Second Army's consolidation.
6. Reserve divisions from each corps were earmarked for phase two: a short final push onto the Oosttaverne Line behind Messines Ridge.

Ypres · Hooge · Stirling Castle · Sanctuary Wood · Zillebeke · Observatory Ridge · N

X XXX MORLAND · 23 XX · Hill 60 · Mount Sorrel · Limit of offensive

24 XX · 47 XX · Ypres–Comines Canal · The Caterpillar · 204 XX · 7 XX · The Bluff

41 XX · St Eloi · White Chateau · Hollebeke · Damm Strasse

19 XX · 35 XX · ④ · ①

IX XXX HAMILTON-GORDON · Vierstraat · Grand Bois

16 XX · 2 XX · Oosttaverne · Gruppe Wytschaete XXX LAFFERT

11 XX · Petit Bois · ③ · Wytschaete · Wambeek

36 XX · ⑤ · Garde-Dieu · 3 BAV XX · ②

40 XX · Messines · Blauwepoortbeek · Gapard · ⑥

Ontario Farm · Hun's Walk

Wulverghem · 25 XX · La Potterie Farm · Warneton

River Douve · NZ XX · 4 BAV XX · River Lys

II XXX ANZAC GODLEY · 4 AUS XX · St Yves · Limit of offensive

Hill 63 · 3 AUS XX · Factory Farm

Ploegsteert Wood

Ploegsteert

–·–·– BEF Corps boundary	——— British front line
——— Red Line – Initial objectives	∿∿∿ Principal German trench systems
——— Blue Line – Intermediate objectives	⋯⋯⋯ Extensive barbed wire systems
——— Green Line – Second intermediate objectives	● Mine
——— Black Line – Phase one culmination	0 —— 1 mile
——— Observation Line – Phase one exploitation	0 —— 1km
——— Oosttaverne Line – Phase two culmination	

bridges beyond the range of Plumer's guns. Fighter units planned to intensify combat air patrols, winning air superiority and hampering German counterbattery survey. The RFC were confident in this; they had as many aircraft over Messines Ridge as General von Armin could muster for his entire front, plus the advantage of a fledgling airborne early-warning network. (Balloon observers took multiple bearings on approaching German aircraft, calculated their location by intersection and vectored fighters.)

Seventy-two of the newly arrived Mark IV tanks were attached to Second Army under command of II Brigade Heavy Branch Machine Gun Corps (precursor to the Tank Corps). Harington kept 24 as an Army-level reserve and allocated the remainder by proportion to forecast difficulty; most were grouped with II ANZAC in the south – 12 to Messines alone.

Plumer placed great emphasis on training, paying close heed to four detailed General Staff doctrine notes produced to capture lessons bought with blood on the Somme. The sculptor Cecil Thomas built a model of Messines Ridge the size of two tennis courts for study by commanders at all levels. Every brigade ran six full-scale dress rehearsals on training areas in French countryside.

Troops examine Second Army's model of Messines Ridge as part of their preparations. It is interesting to see so many junior ranks in this photograph; such briefings were not limited to officers. (IWM E 648)

Deliberate operations of this magnitude create a truly impressive logistic tail. The statistics are worth trying to visualize. During the month of May, Second Army took delivery of 294,000 tonnes of supplies, of which half was artillery ammunition: every 18-pdr had 1,000 rounds of ammunition on the gun-line prior to Zero Hour. 3½ million shells were allocated for the preparatory bombardment. In a bid to reduce road congestion, they laid 185km (115 miles) of broad-gauge railway and 93km (58 miles) of narrow-gauge, some running right up to the heavy gun-lines. By 7 June, Plumer had 31,450 men employed on labour duty alone, building and improving routes for his 9,500-strong motor transport fleet and innumerable pack animals. Anyone in doubt that this was a siege campaign needs to consider that these preparations served a specific objective only 12km (7 miles) wide and 3km (2 miles) deep.

THE BATTLE OF MESSINES

THE WITCH'S CAULDRON

Second Army's preparatory bombardment made a rolling start. 21 May was the official date, but the guns had been more active than normal since May Day; spikes were used to conceal the arrival of supplementary batteries. During the first ten days, Commander Royal Artillery for Second Army, Major-General Franks, applied strict controls over the number of guns that could be unmasked in each corps area.

Around this time, intelligence filtered back to Haig that the Germans were considering withdrawal from Messines Ridge. He was also aware of the *Pioniere* burrowing towards Harvey's charge at Hill 60. On 30 May he called for Plumer and they discussed the options. Haig's recommendation was that the mines should be fired early as a preliminary stroke that would pre-empt any retreat and force the Germans to unmask their battery positions. Plumer held his nerve, arguing that a 'half-cocked' offensive stood a fair chance of being a partial failure. Haig relented, sweetened by the compromise that Plumer would conduct two live dummy runs of the creeping barrage in order to provoke a response from any hidden German batteries.

German artillery fire impacting behind Hill 63 in the first week of June 1917. A crashed British aircraft lies in the foreground. Gruppe Wytschaete's gunners did their best to answer the onslaught but retaliatory shelling only attracted the attention of Plumer's counterbattery concentrations. (IWM E 609)

The following day, Franks opened the floodgates and the weight of fire intensified markedly. With all available weapons in action, Gruppe Wytschaete was assailed from three sides. On 3 and 4 June respectively, Wytschaete and Messines villages received special attention from the heavy guns firing a mix of high-explosive and gas shells. Both were reduced to rubble. Howitzers targeted bridges over the river Lys and Ypres–Comines Canal. Every night, machine-gun barrages rained bullets onto routes used by ration parties; II ANZAC issued 80,000 rounds for this purpose to each division every 24 hours.

The RFC swarmed above and beyond the ridge, strafing rolling stock and dogfighting with plucky German pilots. The area was divided into 'beats' sanitized by fighter aircraft patrolling the German balloon observation line about 10km (6 miles) east of Messines. This kept the battle for air superiority away from the reconnaissance and fire control flights. Karl Schaefer – a German Albatross ace with 30 kills to his name – fell victim to II Brigade's concentration of force that week. Fifty-seven other German aircraft were shot down, at a cost of 33 British machines.

German infantry had to endure the onslaught. Casualties were limited by a prudent order to withdraw men from concrete shelters during the day; pillboxes attracted the attention of heavy guns and men were (ironically) safer in nearby shell holes. But the effect on their nerves was inescapable. Normal five-day rotations in the front were shortened to two. The adjutant of the 2nd Battalion, 4th Grenadier Regiment, up at Wytschaete wrote later about the 'witch's cauldron': 'We were worn down so much that careful watchfulness… gave way to complete indifference. It was all the same to us if we met our fate…. Our situation was desperate.'[21]

Gradually, this state of affairs dawned on the German staff. Just prior to the bombardment intensification, Armin had reported that an attack really was imminent and his situation serious, a message reinforced by Laffert on 4 June when he judged it unlikely that his divisions in the line would hold the outpost zone (whither his earlier confidence?) Yet neither counselled a withdrawal. Hitherto, Arras remained Rupprecht's priority and he was loath to draw down until certain that Haig's focus had shifted. Now he took action, dispatching extra aircraft and artillery. But the order was signed on 6 June – too late. Meanwhile, losses among the 40th Infantry Division around Messines necessitated relief by the 3rd Infantry Division – a process in mid flow when the attack came.

Forty-eight hours in advance of Zero Hour, Franks played his ace card: two major counterbattery concentrations. Plumer's creeping barrage dry runs had paid dividends and goaded many of Laffert's guns into action. A week of beautiful weather had aided the discovery of others that stayed silent. All howitzers with reach – one for every 75m (250ft) of front – focused their attention on 200 identified German gun positions. Gruppe Wytschaete lost half of its heavy artillery and a quarter of its field artillery before a single British infantryman had gone over the top.

FINAL PREPARATIONS

It was not all one-way traffic. British battery concentrations in obvious places like Hill 63 at the west end of Ploegsteert Wood were fired at regularly, often with phosgene gas shells landing with their tell-tale 'plop'. With its distinctive

21. *History of Grenadier Regiment 4*, General Alfred Dietrich, 1928 – translated by Col. Jack Sheldon

Australian infantry idle by the roadside on the eve of battle, 6 June 1917. The troops beyond are making their way to the front. It was a hot and tedious approach march. (IWM E 607)

mouldy hay odour, phosgene kills by attacking the inside of the lungs and causing suffocation. Fortunately for the British gunners, lethal concentrations are hard to achieve with shells – many men were incapacitated but only ten lost their lives during the bombardment.

Second Army HQ set Zero Hour on 6 June once the weather forecast was confirmed: 0310hrs. At this time, mist would be clearing and visibility sufficient at about 100m (330ft). Plumer wanted to have a foothold on the ridge before sunrise at 0441hrs. Only in these last few days did word start to filter out about the mines. Troops needed fair warning to keep down at the moment of detonation. Harington convened a press conference for select correspondents on the eve of the battle. 'Gentlemen', he said, 'I do not know whether or not we shall change history tomorrow but we shall certainly alter geography.'[22]

For the infantry filing into position that night, it was much like any other major attack they might have taken part in. Final briefings in the morning, issue of ammunition, emergency rations and shell dressings. A hearty meal queued for with mixed enthusiasm then the route march to assembly areas. There they waited for darkness before snaking forwards to the front line: some in trenches, others lying out in the open along pre-positioned tapes. A violent evening thunderstorm had given everybody reason to curse. Ploegsteert Wood received a phosgene barrage about the same time. Being heavier than air, the pungent gas clung to the undergrowth, making the 3rd Australian Division's approach march a hellish confusion.

About midnight, the moon revealed itself. They say nightingales could be heard near Wytschaete, where Ulstermen of the 36th Division were about to go into battle for the first time alongside the 16th Division from the south of Ireland. It was warm; many dozed off, helmets resting on forearms. In the enforced silence, a man is imprisoned by his own thoughts and anxieties. At 0230hrs, Plumer knelt by his bed and prayed.

22. *Plumer of Messines*, Gen. Sir Charles Harington, 1935

But none were more anxious than the tunnellers. After so much work and sacrifice, would the mines blow? Some had been down there for a year. Others were only just frantically being primed…. Watches had been carefully synchronized; auxiliary exploders prepared. Up at The Caterpillar, Captain Oliver Woodward from the 1st Australian Tunnelling Company checked and rechecked his firing leads: 'One's nerves seemed to be strained to the breaking point. I approached the task of final testing with a feeling of intense excitement. When each proved correct I felt greatly relieved.'[23]

The final hours and minutes were interminable. Finally, 0300hrs arrived. Woodward continues: 'Breathlessly we watched the minute hand crawl towards ten… Three minutes to go, two to go – one to go – 45 seconds to go – 20 seconds to go – 10 seconds to go… and then FIRE!'[24]

PILLARS OF FIRE

What followed qualifies as the world's largest man-made pre-nuclear explosion. Its report rumbled all the way to London. At Lille University's geology department, the shock wave was mistaken for an earthquake. All 19 mines detonated within the space of 20 seconds.

Some eyewitnesses concede that the scene was indescribable. 'The earth seemed to open up and rise up to the sky. It was all shot with flame.'[25] Lieutenant Brian Frayling was a tunnelling officer at Spanbroekmolen. His testimony is a sound archive, bringing the researcher tantalizingly close to that incredible experience. In clipped tones he recounts the scene: 'The first thing we knew was a terrific tremor of the ground. It was quite fantastic. Sheet flame went up as high as St Paul's [cathedral]; I estimated about 800 feet. It was white incandescent light'.[26]

One firing officer was blown 6m (20ft) along the trench when he pushed down on the exploder. The ground swayed under men's feet – likened by some to a pitching ship. An anonymous tunneller writes that, 'In the pale light, it appeared as if the whole enemy line had begun to dance, then, one after another, huge tongues of flame shot into the air, followed by dense columns of smoke, which flattened out at the top like gigantic mushrooms. From some craters were discharged tremendous showers of sparks rivalling anything ever conceived in the way of fireworks.'[27]

Debris rained down along the front; clods of earth the size of carts landing with an intimidating thud. At Petit Bois, the Inniskilling Fusiliers of 49th Brigade had already launched towards German lines and were caught in the open. The blast wave bowled the lead companies over like skittles and they sustained some casualties from falling spoil.

Curiously, quite a few attest to not hearing anything initially. There was what the Official History describes as a 'ventriloquial' nature to the explosions whereby others thought they had gone off behind British lines. This confusion did not last; as soon as the first mine detonated, Plumer's gunners opened the artillery barrage.

For the first half hour, 265 of the heavier guns fired a third counterbattery concentration with the emphasis on gas attack. Two-thirds of the 18-pdrs

23. Captain O. H. Woodward, quoted in *Beneath Flanders Fields*, Peter Barton et al., 2004
24. Ibid.
25. Captain Martin Greener, IWM Sound Archive Folio 8945
26. Lieutenant Brian Frayling, IWM Sound Archive Folio 4105
27. 'Messines', 'Tunneller' (Anon), *RE Journal*, 1937

Three photographs capture the progress of a mine blast. ABOVE LEFT: the 'push' of the subterranean explosion breaks the surface (practice 'blow', August 1916). ABOVE RIGHT: spoil and debris is sent skyward (Hawthorn Redoubt on the Somme, 1 July 1916). RIGHT: debris settles, leaving a vast pall of dust (Hawthorn Redoubt, minutes later). (IWM Q 79465; 754; 756)

unleashed their creeping barrage just in front of the infantry, each gun firing at a rate of three rounds per minute. This was backed up by two 'standing' barrages: one delivered by the balance of light guns to a depth of 700m (2,300ft) beyond the creeping belt to interdict local counterattack, decimate fleeing troops and further degrade physical defences; the other fired by heavy artillery at enemy rear areas with much the same purpose. A machine-gun barrage filled in the gaps.

Muzzle flashes lit the entire western horizon, setting an orange glow in the night sky such as is today created by the street lights of a large town. A massive pall of smoke and dust settled on the ridge from which emanated innumerable dulled flashes of shell detonations. It was deafening; you feel sound like that as much as hear it.

Attacking infantry needed no order or whistle – it would not be heard. Springing to their feet or clambering hurriedly out of trenches, they were almost beckoned by the angry maelstrom. It shook and pulsed, assailing the

Peckham mine crater as it is today. In June 1917, the crater was 80m (260ft) in diameter and 15m (50ft) deep. The second Peckham charge lost to a German camouflet was located somewhere under the farm in the middle distance. (By kind permission of Lt. Col. Phillip Robinson)

senses with noise, dust and cordite. Bunched together in 'artillery formation' – the diamond shape platoons were now using to maintain order in the advance – they could draw some sense of security from each other. A unique mix of emotions: part trepidation, part elation – either way, humbling. At least one eyewitness recalls sparing a thought for the Germans up on the ridge.

Universally, German accounts place the onslaught shortly after 0400hrs; evidently they were operating on a different time zone. Throughout the night a few units up and down the line were conducting reliefs of forward companies. Many men (including some that later bore testament) owed their lives to this arbitrary administrative churn. One such lucky soul was Fusilier Paul Schumacher of 33rd Fusilier Regiment north of Wytschaete: 'Suddenly there was an enormous flash just where we had come from, to the right by St Eloi and to the left at Messines. Blood red flames shot up into the sky and a dull crack and boom penetrated the roar of the guns. The earth heaved and rocked as though it was trying to tear itself apart.'[28]

Nobody within the blast radius of any mine lived to tell the tale. The largest craters spanned over 80m (260ft), the average being 50–60m (160–200ft). Their 'Diameter of Complete Obliteration' (to quote after-action reports) was up to twice that. Lieutenant Brian Frayling attests that on later inspection of the Spanbroekmolen crater he found no human remains larger than one foot in a boot. There is some contention about how many German soldiers were killed directly by the mines. After the battle, German divisions in the line reported 7,548 men missing for the period 1 to 10 June. This figure appears to be harnessed by some accounts as an indication of mine lethality but that discounts a host of other possibilities (not least a crushing barrage). In the absence of any other evidence, we will never know.

What is clear is that the physical destruction wrought by the mines was of secondary importance to the profound and widespread effect on German cohesion. The 204th Infantry Division's after-action report stated that, '… heavy concrete shelters rocked, a hurricane of hot air from the explosions

28. *33rd Fusilier Regiment in World War 1914–18*, Major Liedtke, 1935 – translated by Col. Jack Sheldon

PILLARS OF FIRE – THE ADVANCE AT PETIT BOIS, 7 JUNE 1917 (pp. 56–57)

The 49th Brigade from the 16th (Irish) Division assaulted the German front lines west of Wytschaete at 0310hrs. Two mines were placed to assist the attack in their sector: Petit Bois I and II. It was essentially still dark at this time and the illustration has sought to replicate light levels as accurately as possible; ground mist was starting to lift and visibility just before Zero Hour was about 50–100m (165–330ft). Some accounts report that troops were ordered out of jump-off trenches through fear that sides would collapse when the mines went off but this is not consistent – and in areas like Petit Bois where opposing lines were close, it is likely that local commanders would have taken their chances rather than risk casualties from harassing artillery by lying in the open. Lead battalions from the 49th Brigade exited at 0310hrs precisely and the first wave made rapid progress across no man's land in 'artillery formation' – the diamond-shaped platoon disposition that most favoured cohesion at times like this when command and control was difficult. Unfortunately, the two mines detonated 12 seconds late, catching forward platoons in the open. They didn't wait because commanders were operating to precise artillery timetables and so forged ahead on the assumption that the mines had failed to blow (setbacks like that were all too familiar to veterans). As it was, the force of the blast threw men off their feet (1); its circular pulse – like a pond ripple – would have been visible in the thin, low-lying mist (2). Readers familiar with archive footage taken by bomb aimers will have seen this effect emanating from ordnance impacting on the ground. The spectacle was so awe-inspiring that many of those present later conceded it was 'indescribable'. Columns of smoke, dust and flame rose majestically nearly a thousand feet into the air (3) before raining spoil (4) that proved lethal not just to the German front-line garrison but also 49th Brigade infantrymen that had strayed too close. The largest chunks – some weighing several tonnes – must have been terrifying to men so devoid of cover. Everything beneath their feet shook like an earthquake. But momentum was essential; the mines had created a valuable tactical advantage and officers exhorted the men forwards regardless (5). Within seconds, Second Army's massive artillery concentration was in action and the assaulting battalions had to keep within the protective curtain of their creeping barrage. Eyewitnesses recall that the innumerable shell detonations flashed from within the dust like lightning in a storm cloud, the net effect of which was a steady glow settled on the horizon (6).

The fury and relentlessness of Second Army's creeping barrage is difficult to evoke. This remarkable image of German shellfire at Messines might help. The proximity of the camera proves how close one can be and still emerge unscathed. Following a barrage, one is assisted by the trajectory of shells which throws the shrapnel forwards. (IWM E 599)

swept back for many kilometres, dropping fragments of wood, iron and earth; black clouds of smoke and dust spread over the country. The effect on the troops was overpowering and crushing.'[29]

Gruppe Wytschaete's outpost zone was completely neutralized; those that survived the mines and barrage were either wounded or stunned. Advancing British troops encountered sentries and outpost detachments 'cringing like beaten animals [and making]... fruitless attempts to embrace us'.[30] Plumer had planned for a simultaneous detonation; the fact that the mines went off in rapid sequence actually enhanced the trauma. Even sectors where mines were absent (such as Petite Douve and The Bluff) failed to mount resistance in the outpost zone – a testament to the fury of the barrage, described by German soldiers as relentless 'drumfire'.

SOS flares arced haphazardly into the gloom but Laffert's gun-lines were slow to respond; many did not answer at all. It took between five and ten minutes for shells to start falling on the British front line.

By this time the lead battalions were well on their way. Planners grossly underestimated the obscuration from mine blasts and shelling, exacerbated by artillery smoke tasks to screen off defilade positions at The Bluff and Ontario Farm. Visibility was less than half what they had expected; mine craters caused muddling changes of direction. This is where rehearsals paid off; platoons used pre-arranged compass bearings and knew what features they were looking for.

Inexorably, the creeping barrage staggered up the ridge, lifting 100m (330ft) every two minutes. Infantry pushed on after it – sometimes as close as *20m (65ft)* – 'mopping' detachments clearing deep dugouts and processing prisoners of war behind them. As dawn blushed the eastern horizon, they arrived at their first objective line – less than 40 minutes after Zero Hour and, thus far, virtually unopposed. The two lead battalions in each brigade were now leapfrogged by fresh legs, ready to push onto the German second line 800m (½ a mile) up the slope.

29. Quoted in British Official History, *Messines and Third Ypres 1917*, Brig. Gen. Sir James Edmonds, 1948

30. Lieutenant W. L. Garrard, 40th Bn. Royal Australian Regiment, quoted in *Official History of Australia in the War of 1914–1918*, C. E. W. Bean, 1929

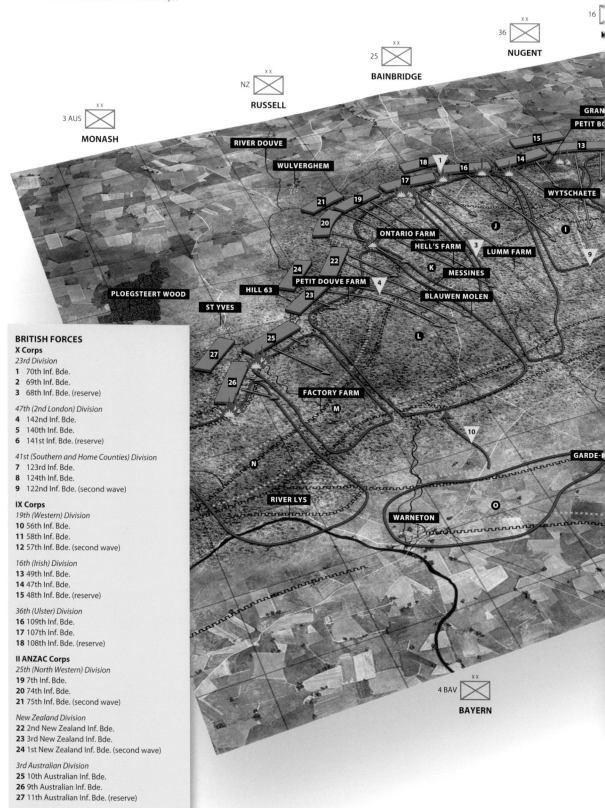

Note: Gridlines are shown at intervals of 1km/1093yds

16

36 NUGENT

25 BAINBRIDGE

NZ RUSSELL

3 AUS MONASH

RIVER DOUVE

WULVERGHEM

GRAN
PETIT B

15

13

18 1

17 16

14

WYTSCHAETE

21 19

20

J

I

9

ONTARIO FARM

HELL'S FARM 3 LUMM FARM

K MESSINES

22

24 PETIT DOUVE FARM 4

HILL 63 23 BLAUWEN MOLEN

ST YVES

PLOEGSTEERT WOOD

L

25

27

FACTORY FARM

26 M

10

GARDE-

N

RIVER LYS

O

WARNETON

4 BAV BAYERN

BRITISH FORCES

X Corps

23rd Division
1 70th Inf. Bde.
2 69th Inf. Bde.
3 68th Inf. Bde. (reserve)

47th (2nd London) Division
4 142nd Inf. Bde.
5 140th Inf. Bde.
6 141st Inf. Bde. (reserve)

41st (Southern and Home Counties) Division
7 123rd Inf. Bde.
8 124th Inf. Bde.
9 122nd Inf. Bde. (second wave)

IX Corps

19th (Western) Division
10 56th Inf. Bde.
11 58th Inf. Bde.
12 57th Inf. Bde. (second wave)

16th (Irish) Division
13 49th Inf. Bde.
14 47th Inf. Bde.
15 48th Inf. Bde. (reserve)

36th (Ulster) Division
16 109th Inf. Bde.
17 107th Inf. Bde.
18 108th Inf. Bde. (reserve)

II ANZAC Corps

25th (North Western) Division
19 7th Inf. Bde.
20 74th Inf. Bde.
21 75th Inf. Bde. (second wave)

New Zealand Division
22 2nd New Zealand Inf. Bde.
23 3rd New Zealand Inf. Bde.
24 1st New Zealand Inf. Bde. (second wave)

3rd Australian Division
25 10th Australian Inf. Bde.
26 9th Australian Inf. Bde.
27 11th Australian Inf. Bde. (reserve)

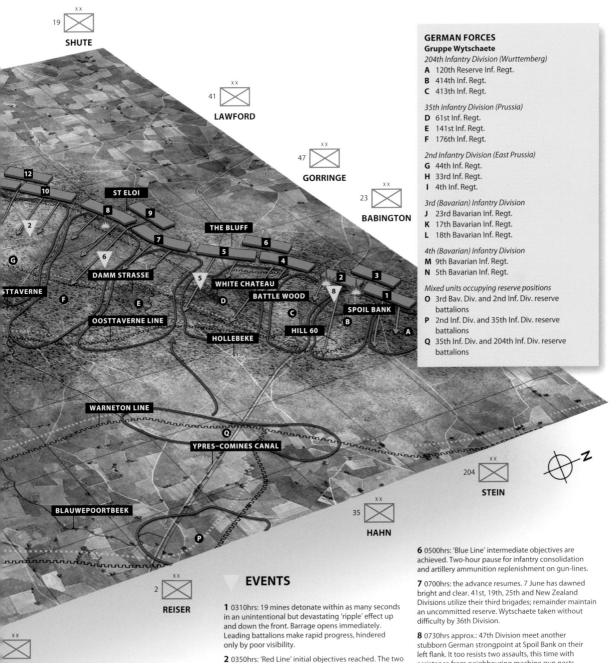

GERMAN FORCES
Gruppe Wytschaete
204th Infantry Division (Wurttemberg)
A 120th Reserve Inf. Regt.
B 414th Inf. Regt.
C 413th Inf. Regt.

35th Infantry Division (Prussia)
D 61st Inf. Regt.
E 141st Inf. Regt.
F 176th Inf. Regt.

2nd Infantry Division (East Prussia)
G 44th Inf. Regt.
H 33rd Inf. Regt.
I 4th Inf. Regt.

3rd (Bavarian) Infantry Division
J 23rd Bavarian Inf. Regt.
K 17th Bavarian Inf. Regt.
L 18th Bavarian Inf. Regt.

4th (Bavarian) Infantry Division
M 9th Bavarian Inf. Regt.
N 5th Bavarian Inf. Regt.

Mixed units occupying reserve positions
O 3rd Bav. Div. and 2nd Inf. Div. reserve battalions
P 2nd Inf. Div. and 35th Inf. Div. reserve battalions
Q 35th Inf. Div. and 204th Inf. Div. reserve battalions

Map labels: SHUTE, LAWFORD, GORRINGE, BABINGTON, ST ELOI, THE BLUFF, DAMM STRASSE, WHITE CHATEAU, BATTLE WOOD, SPOIL BANK, OOSTTAVERNE, OOSTTAVERNE LINE, HOLLEBEKE, HILL 60, WARNETON LINE, YPRES–COMINES CANAL, BLAUWEPOORTBEEK, STEIN, HAHN, REISER, NNINGER, 204, 35, 2, 19, 41, 47, 23

EVENTS

1 0310hrs: 19 mines detonate within as many seconds in an unintentional but devastating 'ripple' effect up and down the front. Barrage opens immediately. Leading battalions make rapid progress, hindered only by poor visibility.

2 0350hrs: 'Red Line' initial objectives reached. The two lead battalions in each brigade make way for the fresh supporting battalions behind them. First light.

3 0400hrs +: some German strongpoints and forward command posts (KTK) resist the renewed advance, in many cases refusing to surrender and requiring bypass to maintain schedule.

4 0420hrs: New Zealanders breach the outer defences of Messines and converge on the village square. Strongpoints are subdued by smoke bombs and the tenacity of small units.

5 0430hrs approx.: 47th Division is held up by the German strongpoint at White Chateau. It resists the first two assaults and is not vanquished until 0750hrs.

6 0500hrs: 'Blue Line' intermediate objectives are achieved. Two-hour pause for infantry consolidation and artillery ammunition replenishment on gun-lines.

7 0700hrs: the advance resumes. 7 June has dawned bright and clear. 41st, 19th, 25th and New Zealand Divisions utilize their third brigades; remainder maintain an uncommitted reserve. Wytschaete taken without difficulty by 36th Division.

8 0730hrs approx.: 47th Division meet another stubborn German strongpoint at Spoil Bank on their left flank. It too resists two assaults, this time with assistance from neighbouring machine gun nests in Battle Wood firing from defilade. British pull back at 0900hrs to soften Spoil Bank with artillery.

9 0840hrs: arrival at 'Black Line' heralds culmination of phase one objectives. Leading companies clear beyond to the 'Observation Line' in order to provide early warning of any German counterattack. Consolidating troops dig in under an increasingly hot sun.

10 Gruppe Wytschaete's only forward movement of the morning has been passage of reserve units to the vicinity of Oosttaverne Line (Sehnen Stellung). Arriving at approximately 0730hrs, *Eingreif* divisions were placed under the battlefield command of divisions in the line and warned off for counterattack.

THE BATTLE OF MESSINES RIDGE

7 June 1917, British Second Army (IV Corps) phase one advances viewed from the South, 0310hrs to 0900hrs

CONCRETE CRYPTS

It was a tough morning to be a *Kampftruppenkommandeur* (KTK). Roused by the earthquake, KTKs passed the first hour trying desperately to piece a battle picture together. Field telephone communication with forward companies had ceased abruptly with the onset of attack. The 413th Infantry Regiment's KTK command post up on Hill 60 employed two message dogs: one returned wounded and the other refused to leave. Runners were the only option. After a short time these breathless, panic-stricken harbingers started to arrive at command posts up and down the line. '… Swarms of enemy infantry carpeting the ridge…. Whole companies consumed by mine blasts…. No word from neighbouring battalions…'

It did not take long for these commanders to realize that their battalions had effectively ceased to exist. Retreating stragglers – some in a demented state – were in no way fit to be incorporated into support line garrisons. Instead *Gegenstoss* detachments from the reserve line were hurried forwards to assist with the defence of these strongpoints, running the gauntlet of Second Army's unremitting barrage.

There was little more that the KTKs could do; support and reserve battalions had their own command posts and the forward battle was already lost. A few withdrew. But this was anathema to others, emotional at the demise of their troops. One such lion was the KTK at Thümmelschloss, a concrete blockhouse acting as command post for III Battalion, 17th Bavarian Infantry Regiment, based north of Messines. 'Major von Kohlmüller blanched as he absorbed the news that his beloved battalion had been destroyed. But, a moment later, he opened his mouth and said firmly, "all personnel in Thümmelschloss listen to my orders… I have been brought up to hold the position with which I have been entrusted. We are either going to die here or be relieved… I am not pulling out!"'[31]

Tenacity of this kind changed the character of Second Army's advance after the initial objective line. No infantry force could have resisted Plumer's awesome curtain-raiser but Laffert's *Feldgrauen* were a tough and stoic breed. When given half a chance, they put up a fight.

Down at the southern end of the ridge, II ANZAC was converging on Messines. Despite the village's wholesale battering by heavy guns (a process that had continued all morning), the defences were in adequate condition.

31. *History of Bavarian Regiment 17*, Hauptmann Johann Riegel, 1927 – translated by Col. Jack Sheldon

A conventional trench system on the outskirts was backed up by five concrete strongpoints and a network of deep dugouts in the centre, all manned by two companies of the 18th Bavarian Infantry Regiment.

Messines itself was a task for Major-General Andrew Russell's New Zealand Division. He had Australians to his south and the British 25th Division further up towards Wytschaete. It was well understood that Messines might impede them so the creeping barrage slowed to a lift rate of 100m (330ft) every 11 minutes. Three machine-gun positions on the outer ring caused some trouble initially; one in a farm building north of Messines was silenced by a Mk. IV tank driving through the wall. The other two were overcome by the dash and initiative of Lance-Corporal Samuel Frickleton from 3rd New Zealand Rifle Battalion. Spying their location from afar, he led his section actually into the barrage, which was still settled on that locality. Both Maxims were destroyed with grenades. Frickleton was later awarded a Victoria Cross.

The Kiwis were soon into the village. Here a brutal and confused battle unfolded amid the rubble. It was still quite dark as the sun had yet to rise into view. War diaries describe a 'disorganized' Bavarian defence but this kind of fighting is ever thus: a mêlée decided by the sum of individual acts. It is easy to evoke in one's mind – the cacophony of shouts, small-arms fire and grenades with their distinctive bass 'HHUNK'; machine-gun fire slapping into masonry and ricocheting around with an ascending whine; pallid bleeding men being dragged into cover and stripped of equipment while the next section clambers over them in a tangle of limbs, barking at one another. One by one the strongpoints fell, some subdued by smoke grenades that forced defenders to emerge, choking, into the open where they were cut down or rounded up. Hauptmann Thomas, the German commander, was captured along with his staff in a bunker near the church ruins.

Somewhere north of Messines was the Thümmelschloss, where Kohlmüller and his men continued their resistance against 'several companies' that attacked at 0600hrs (British time): 'This developed into hand to hand fighting, during which Major von Kohlmüller set a shining example to all. The attack was beaten back several times but this had cost us much blood. Only five lightly wounded officers, two machine guns and a few men remained to give battle.'[32]

Soon after, a shell killed Kohlmüller and the next attack silenced the Thümmelschloss at last. It is possible that this action was what the 25th Division described as a 'sharp fight' at Hell's Farm, 700m (2,300ft) north-west of Messines. No other episode in 17th Bavarian Infantry Regiment's sector fits the description.

By contrast, IX Corps made businesslike progress through their area of operations. The Ulstermen of the 36th Division picked their way across ground 'ploughed' by artillery shells.

North-west of Wytschaete village, the 16th and 19th Divisions had encountered few difficulties in the shattered remnants of Wytschaete Wood and Grand Bois respectively. Both had been subjected to incendiary attack during the preparatory bombardment. Only a strongpoint at the northern extremity of Wytschaete Wood – known as L'Hospice – caused serious trouble and refused to surrender. It was bypassed and handed over to 'mopping' units who forced its capitulation shortly before 0700hrs.

32. Ibid.

At the uppermost part of the ridge, X Corps had their sights on two probable hotspots of note: the levelled drive 'Damm Strasse' and its one-time destination, White Chateau. Both were veritable warrens that small bands of men would have little difficulty in defending effectively. Moreover, Gruppe Wytschaete had a higher density of defenders in this region than anywhere else on Messines Ridge: two divisions for a 6km (4-mile) frontage.

Damm Strasse proved less trouble than Major-General Lawford's 41st Division had feared, predominantly because of the intense preparatory and creeping barrages. Private Fagence of 11th Battalion, Queen's Royal West Surrey Regiment, was in the first wave: 'I remember crossing the Damm Strasse, which had been considerably smashed up by our shell-fire. There were scores of dead Germans strewn around; some of the bodies were in grotesque positions but we had no time to stop and look.'[33]

White Chateau had more in store for the Londoners of the 47th Division. Their approach had been shielded by a thick smokescreen but as the Chateau came into view (by this stage of the war a high rubble pile interspersed with pillboxes) they were met by a withering fire. Private Frank Dunham was there with the 1/7th Battalion London Regiment:

> It had been reduced to a large heap of broken masonry over the cellars. Our company made an unsuccessful attempt to capture [it] as the enemy had a number of machine guns... and these opened fire immediately the troops attempted to close in. Then the 6th Londons appeared on the scene. One of their leading company commanders... was strolling about the battlefield, carrying his cane and wearing a monocle. As he came level with our company he shouted, "haven't you captured this bally place yet?"
> *Quoted in* Pillars of Fire, *Ian Passingham, 1998*

A second attack also failed so Stokes trench mortars arrived to soften it up. Next the 6th and 7th Londons tried a combined attack. One British sergeant-major is reported to have scaled the rubble heap and thrown two grenades at a machine-gun nest beyond. His pouches empty, he then chucked bricks instead and directed a flanking advance by waving from his vantage point. Against such foolhardy opposition, the 64-strong garrison surrendered.

Meanwhile, at approximately 0500hrs, the remainder of Second Army had gained the intermediate objective. This called for a scheduled two-hour pause to permit ammunition replenishment and barrel cooling on gun-lines. Mopping operations continued back in Messines, Damm Strasse and White Chateau (which did not fall until 0750hrs).

7 June dawned clear; though still cool, the air had that thick quality that tells you it's going to be hot. Four of the nine attacking divisions used the opportunity to push fresh brigades into the advance; others elected to drive on with their reserve uncommitted. Troops did not sit idle; experience hewn from previous bruising encounters dictated the imperative for consolidation. Pack mules, divisional pioneer battalions and reserve units brought forwards defence stores and ammunition to assist in this frenetic effort. Private Fagence recalls: 'It didn't matter how tired you were. You dug as fast as you could, because it was a matter of life and death to get some protection against enemy shell-fire.'[34]

33. Quoted in *They called it Passchendaele*, Lyn Macdonald, 1978
34. Ibid.

Field artillery batteries on creeping barrage duty reduced their rate of fire to one round per minute, creating a 300m (1,000ft) zone of fire beyond the consolidation line. Tanks that had been outstripped by advancing infantry over difficult ground had a chance to catch up.

At 0700hrs precisely, the barrage stepped up again and Second Army's advance resumed. Phase one culmination (Black Line) was only 800m ($^1/_2$ a mile) further on.

The ANZACs swept over the German artillery coordination HQ at Blauwen Molen (a now defunct windmill) and captured 100 *Feldgrauen* at a strongpoint known as Fanny's Farm after a Mk. IV knocked a few holes in the wall with its 6-pdrs. A cluster of bunkers near Lumm Farm put up stiff resistance in the manner of Thümmelschloss. It sat right on the corps boundary between the 25th and 36th Divisions, hence there is confusion in war diaries as to who can claim it.

TOP
Infantrymen from the 36th (Ulster) Division pick their way through the rubble of Wytschaete. Much of the damage was wrought during the preparatory barrage. Unlike Messines, this strongpoint capitulated without incident. (IWM Q 5460)

BOTTOM
The forlorn remains of Oosttaverne Wood in June 1917. Whenever you read about 'woods' during Great War battles, remember that this is often what they looked like. Plumer's 'Observation Line' lay just beyond. (IWM Q 2304)

In prospect, Wytschaete village threatened a repeat of the grubby business at Messines – its defences were configured in a similar way. Fortunately for the lead brigades of the 16th Division, it fell with only slight resistance: the one functioning machine-gun nest was overcome by a tank. Preparatory bombardment had reduced it to a sea of bricks and splintered roof timbers. Indeed, aside from Lumm Farm, IX Corps had an almost pedestrian progress to Black Line.

Akin to White Chateau, it was X Corps that had their work cut out. The 47th Division were tasked with 'Spoil Bank' – another of the Belgian civil engineering by-products in the area. This 400m-long (1,300ft) mound ran north of the canal and had machine-gun emplacements dug into its flanks almost like a Georgian warship's cannon. The 142nd Brigade sent the Surrey Rifles and Queen's Battalions of the London Regiment on two costly attempts at Spoil Bank, succeeding only in creating a lodgement at its western end. Matters were complicated by enfilade fire from nearby Battle Wood. The brigade withdrew after two hours so that the objective could be worked over by artillery. In fact its tenacious Prussian defenders were reinforced and still held out 24 hours later.

Battle Wood was the 23rd Division's objective for the morning. As is evident from the garrison's contribution to the defence of Spoil Bank, Major-General Babington's men also struggled to maintain schedule. In this case it was the trench systems east of Mount Sorrell that slowed things down. The 70th Brigade on this left flank did not complete their consolidation until the evening. Elsewhere, X Corps benefited from the capitulation of White Chateau; the 41st Division had a relatively easy run up to Black Line.

By 0840hrs, the Black Line had been carried from south of Spoil Bank all the way down to Factory Farm. In the centre between Wytschaete and Messines, the creeping barrage covered leading infantry companies and eight tanks down the convex slope to Plumer's 'Observation Line', clearing Oosttaverne Wood and some reserve line dugouts of enemy stragglers. Phase one was complete.

BELLEVUE

At this juncture, Second Army's operation exceeded expectations. The hiccup at Spoil Bank and delays around White Chateau are conspicuous only because it was such an unqualified success elsewhere on the front: four battalions held up out of over a hundred in the advance. The operation had run like clockwork. Furthermore, relative to their experience of previous offensives, casualty rates during phase one were nigh on miraculous – on average under 5 per cent. When Harington broke the news to Plumer that Messines Ridge was in British hands, he remembers a hand being placed on his shoulder and tears in the venerable general's eyes.

Accustomed as they were to the desolate landscape of Ypres Salient, the vista from atop Messines Ridge was a marvel rendered all the sweeter by such a glorious morning. Grassland dipped away into the dead ground of the convex slope but then beyond, emerging from haze, the Lys River valley stretched out. There were lush fields, hedgerows, sleepy villages and woods thick with leaves. One officer likened it to a picnic spot.

But they were at war and this was the point where they expected concerted and well-rehearsed counterattack by *Eingreif* divisions. Shedding their tunics, the men set about digging with determined urgency.

Here Second Army paid for its own success. Extrapolation of past casualty statistics for attack frontages of this density had produced forecasts of approximately 50 per cent for phase one. Thus there were nearly twice as many men crowding the front line than had been planned for. Enemy artillery and machine guns soon ranged in to take advantage of the density; there was nothing to do but dig faster. One Maori pioneer company in New Zealand Division took just one hour to spade 2m (7ft) deep.

German gunners did not have it all their own way; such a clear morning also favoured the RFC. Circling like hungry gulls, a plethora of aircraft types joined in what one RFC historian describes as 'low level mayhem': 'Second Lieutenant Barlow... dived at a German aerodrome and peppered the hangars from twenty feet, spotted a nearby train and hosed it with both Vickers and Lewis, and riddled rolling stock in the nearby station yard. He still had enough ammunition – and aggression – to perforate the sheds of a second aerodrome on his way home.'[35]

35. *The Royal Flying Corps in World War I*, Ralph Barker, 1995

British wounded resting at a forward dressing station. They are waiting for the arrival of ambulances to convey them to a field hospital. Awnings are to shield them from the baking sun of 7 June. At this stage of the battle, some units had barely sustained any casualties. (IWM Q 5473)

Gun-lines, rear area defensive positions and retreating forces also suffered at the hands of the RFC. German eyewitness accounts of 7 June abound with references to 'birds of prey'.

Back on the start-line, tunnelling officers ambled forwards to inspect their handiwork. Formally mandated to survey German dugouts and pillboxes, the exploration afforded an opportunity to discover exactly what Füsslein and his *Pioniere* had achieved below ground. German workings were extensive, though nothing within 250m (820ft) of any crater survived collapse. Most heartening of all was how accurate listening posts proved to have been in their deductions about German networks.

Around them the ridge was a hive of activity. Phase one completion was the trigger for a multitude of logistic and engineering tasks: chiefly plank road construction and route repair to open arteries up to the new front line. In advance of these slow-moving tentacles were the pack animals and labour companies, tasked (as previously that morning) with ferrying forward supplies for consolidation. Canadian-designed 'Yukon' packs proved their worth here – effectively an early form of external rigid frame rucksack that enabled loads in excess of 30kg (65lb).

As an example, machine-gun companies utilized Yukon-equipped fatigue parties to ferry ammunition belts at Messines. In addition to a Yukon, bearers were given four sandbags to sling over their shoulders containing one 250-round belt box each – that's equivalent to about four large bags of potatoes. Consider how hot it was and the effort required to lug this burden 4km (2 miles) up onto the ridge across what was effectively a ploughed field covered in deep shell holes... they then turned around and repeated the exercise until someone told them to stop. Soldiering is replete with such Sisyphean labours; oaths proliferate.

Originally, there was to be no pause at the Black Line: no chance for Gruppe Wytschaete to get organized. But experience dictated that breaks were justified – and always preferable to enforced delay. Better to run things on your terms. Consequently, Plumer and his corps commanders settled on a five-hour hiatus. On the day however, logistic units conducting the resupply effort up onto the ridge soon reported the broken state of the ground. Plumer

decided to account for this with another two hours on the timetable, delaying phase two until 1510hrs – exactly 12 hours after his original Zero.

Behind the consolidating infantry, tapes and flags were laid out marking assembly areas for three reserve divisions tasked with undertaking the final act: the 4th Australian Division from II ANZAC, 11th Division on IX Corps' central axis and 24th Division in the north under X Corps.

GEGENSTOSS

In the meantime, it was Laffert's move. The speed and ferocity of Second Army's onslaught shattered all of his planning assumptions: the forward zone had held for barely one hour, let alone the 12 he had in mind. In addition, his two specialist *Eingreif* formations – the 3rd and 35th Infantry Divisions, trained and rehearsed in the role – had been forced into the line as relief for garrison units exhausted by weeks of preparatory shelling. Replacing them were the 1st Guards Reserve Division in the south, billeted around Wervicq, and 7th Infantry Division in the north, based outside Menin. These two formations were being set up to fail.

On 3 June, Armin had decided to move the 7th Infantry Division from Houthem (about 10km [6 miles] behind the front line) up to Gheluvelt. He feared that impending attack on Messines Ridge would be followed swiftly by a second axis on the Ypres–Menin road. By moving the 7th Infantry Division further north, Armin hedged his bets. With hindsight it is easy to criticize: this revised disposition gave the 7th Infantry Division an extra 8km (5 miles) to march in support of Gruppe Wytschaete. However, historians would be quick to credit his vision if the 7th Infantry Division had interdicted a subsidiary thrust towards Menin. Armin had to make do with a shortage of infantry divisions. The dice fell differently. The 7th Infantry Division were stood to within minutes of the mines going up and could not be released until 0700hrs (British time) when Armin was confident that he faced only one axis.

The 1st Guards Reserve Division also received their marching orders in the early hours of the morning and made for Garde-Dieu. Their handicap was the fact that units were still detraining having arrived from Arras that night. Company commanders had never seen the ground and passed vital hours getting briefed. With the western sky aglow and battle rumbling away, a few cynical comments will have been shared between officers as they managed the nocturnal pandemonium.

Therefore at sunrise on 7 June Laffert had a few reserve battalions holding the Oosttaverne Line and two unfamiliar and ill-prepared divisions still a considerable distance to the rear. Milling around in between were the pathetic remnants of his forward battalions and columns of weary Saxons from the 40th Infantry Division who thought they were heading for rest billets in Warneton.

The inherently aggressive spirit of his *Feldgrauen* had given rise to some notable last stands and localized (futile) attempts at counterattack but ethos alone cannot be the anchor for an area defence. Events were exceeding Laffert's grasp.

With *Eingreifentaktik*, timing was everything – make the vital counterstroke just as the enemy had overextended himself. Ideally, regiments engaged in battle and able to read the situation cued this. Gruppe Wytschaete's chain of command had been dislocated by the rapid destruction of its forward battalions. There was no situational awareness to speak of. Hence the folly of 5th Bavarian Reserve Regiment's 0700hrs orders to recapture the ridge between Douve and Messines. Moving forwards an hour later, it was immediately obvious that this was impossible; instead they reinforced the Oosttaverne Line.

Germans differentiated between *Gegenstoss* (as explained) and *Gegenangriff* – a deliberate counterattack with days of planning, artillery preparation etc. Had Laffert enjoyed a better appreciation of Second Army achievements and resources, he may not have bothered with the former – two divisions turning up late to strike a consolidated force at least three times their number. Of course one can understand the urgency; conventional wisdom favours rapid counterattack before an opponent has invested himself. Laffert was blind. The crushing limits of communications technology in the Great War affected both sides. Be that as it may, his situation probably called for *Gegenangriff* and even then, only after careful consideration.

The 1st Guards Reserve Division turned up first. Under the *Gruppen* system, they reported to 3rd (Bavarian) Infantry Division in the line, who ordered their lead regiment to attack astride Messines and roll back the British to their original front line. Evidently, General von Wenninger wore a similar blindfold in the information vacuum. The operation was disastrous – Plumer's ambush sprung. Crossing the Oosttaverne Line at 1345hrs on a 1,000m (3,300ft) frontage south of Blauwepoortbeek, the waves of infantry ran into well sited machine guns and a preregistered artillery barrage. Just three in ten men returned unscathed. Consequently, the remaining two regiments were held back on the Warneton Line.

Literally doubling down the road in a muck sweat, the 7th Infantry Division were making up for lost time. Placed under the orders of Generalleutnant Meister's 2nd Infantry Division, their optimistic mission was a simultaneous advance on Wytschaete. Once observed, the British called in a barrage of 6in. and 60-pdr heavy artillery rounds that ranged up and down 7th Infantry Division's infernal route march. Hard pressed around Mount Sorrell and Spoil Bank, the 35th Infantry Division came to their rescue, diverting the lead regiment into assisting with defence. By the time the remaining two reached the 2nd Infantry Division, it was too late to mount an attack and the regiments were depleted by shellfire.

In the final analysis, Laffert had made a *Gegenstoss* of sorts: the Oosttaverne Line was significantly reinforced. Everyone awaited Plumer's inevitable lunge.

SCENE OF A FAMOUS FIGHT

Communications difficulties complicated life for the 4th Australian Division as well. After a long approach, they arrived at the old British front line around 1100hrs, a better place to wait than the Observation Line where there was precious little cover. Typically, the message about Plumer's delay did not reach them in time so they slogged on up to their taped assembly boxes and passed an afternoon lying in the open under bombardment. It is a perfect vignette for convoluted Great War battlefield communications: divisional HQ was telephoned at 1030hrs, relayed the message by field telephone to the forward tactical HQ of New Zealand Division (itself a significant achievement as that line had been dragged forwards in the attack's wake) who then sent runners back down the hill to interdict the Australians moving forwards, by which time they had arrived. All very interesting from a historical perspective, way beyond the comprehension of young infantrymen wondering who on earth had arranged their murderous siesta.

One is minded that perhaps Plumer's delay validates the aphorism 'order plus counterorder equals disorder'. But then it transpires that the 11th Division's single attacking brigade (33rd) needed every last minute to get into position. Without delay, their axis would have been a total shambles. A similar catalogue of communications frictions abounded. As it was, the 19th Division showed admirable flexibility and initiative, lending them its one uncommitted reserve brigade (57th), who initiated the assault on schedule.

Laffert's two *Eingreif* divisions were not trained in the role and lacked familiarity with Messines. Nevertheless, they endeavoured to get forwards – in the 7th Infantry Division's case, all the way from Gheluvelt. This photograph was taken in July 1917 but similar scenes were unfolding on 7 June. (IWM Q 68035)

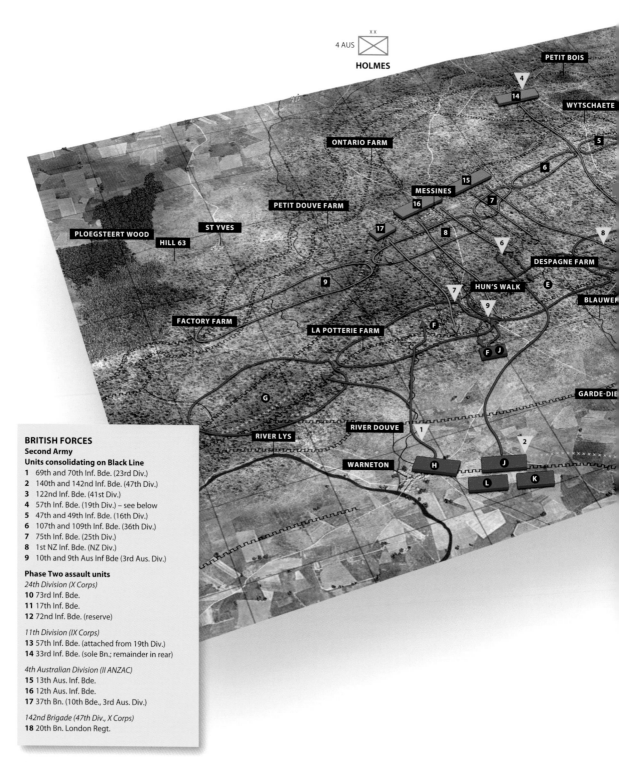

BRITISH FORCES
Second Army
Units consolidating on Black Line
1   69th and 70th Inf. Bde. (23rd Div.)
2   140th and 142nd Inf. Bde. (47th Div.)
3   122nd Inf. Bde. (41st Div.)
4   57th Inf. Bde. (19th Div.) – see below
5   47th and 49th Inf. Bde. (16th Div.)
6   107th and 109th Inf. Bde. (36th Div.)
7   75th Inf. Bde. (25th Div.)
8   1st NZ Inf. Bde. (NZ Div.)
9   10th and 9th Aus Inf Bde (3rd Aus. Div.)

Phase Two assault units
24th Division (X Corps)
10 73rd Inf. Bde.
11 17th Inf. Bde.
12 72nd Inf. Bde. (reserve)

11th Division (IX Corps)
13 57th Inf. Bde. (attached from 19th Div.)
14 33rd Inf. Bde. (sole Bn.; remainder in rear)

4th Australian Division (II ANZAC)
15 13th Aus. Inf. Bde.
16 12th Aus. Inf. Bde.
17 37th Bn. (10th Bde., 3rd Aus. Div.)

142nd Brigade (47th Div., X Corps)
18 20th Bn. London Regt.

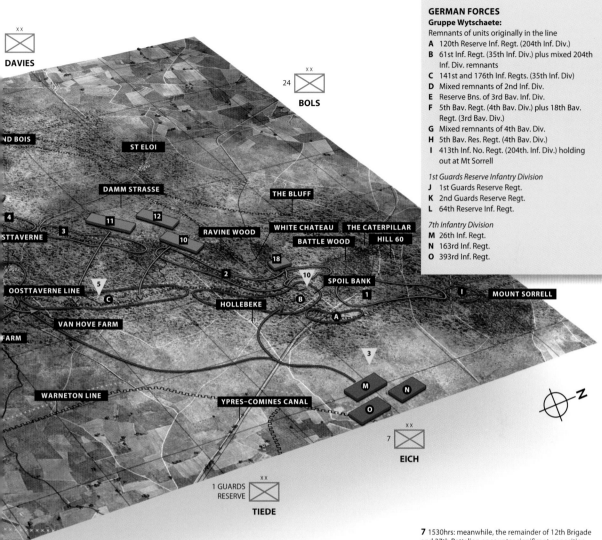

GERMAN FORCES

Gruppe Wytschaete:

Remnants of units originally in the line

A 120th Reserve Inf. Regt. (204th Inf. Div.)
B 61st Inf. Regt. (35th Inf. Div.) plus mixed 204th Inf. Div. remnants
C 141st and 176th Inf. Regts. (35th Inf. Div)
D Mixed remnants of 2nd Inf. Div.
E Reserve Bns. of 3rd Bav. Inf. Div.
F 5th Bav. Regt. (4th Bav. Div.) plus 18th Bav. Regt. (3rd Bav. Div.)
G Mixed remnants of 4th Bav. Div.
H 5th Bav. Res. Regt. (4th Bav. Div.)
I 413th Inf. No. Regt. (204th. Inf. Div.) holding out at Mt Sorrell

1st Guards Reserve Infantry Division

J 1st Guards Reserve Regt.
K 2nd Guards Reserve Regt.
L 64th Reserve Inf. Regt.

7th Infantry Division

M 26th Inf. Regt.
N 163rd Inf. Regt.
O 393rd Inf. Regt.

EVENTS

1 0900hrs: 5th Bavarian Reserve Regiment is ordered to retake the ridge between Messines and river Douve. Seeing the folly of it immediately, they reinforce Oosttaverne Line.

2 1345hrs: having arrived from Arras overnight, 1st Guards Reserve Division comes under 3rd (Bavarian) Infantry Division and are ordered to counterattack south of Blauwepoortbeek. Their lead regiment is decimated. Remainder reinforces Oosttaverne Line.

3 1300–1700hrs: not released from Gheluvelt until 0700hrs, 7th Infantry Division arrives from 1300hrs, crossing the canal under heavy bombardment. Lead regiment is fed up to Spoil Bank under 35th Infantry Division; remainder fill out defences north of Wambeek.

4 1400hrs: owing to a communications failure, 33rd Brigade is late moving forward to assembly areas for phase two. On hearing about the delay, 19th Division commits its reserve brigade (57th) to the task.

5 1510hrs: the northern half of the Oosttaverne Line poses no difficulties for 24th Division's attacking brigades – one battalion only sustains six casualties. 57th Brigade also sweeps through Oosttaverne village virtually unopposed.

6 1530hrs: Blauwepoortbeek Valley is split between 12th and 13th Australian Brigades. Both attacking battalions are stopped 500m short of the Oosttaverne Line by well-sited machine guns and field artillery in the direct fire role.

7 1530hrs: meanwhile, the remainder of 12th Brigade and 37th Battalion encounter significant opposition from a network of pillboxes picketing the Oosttaverne Line astride Hun's Walk. Having overcome this obstacle, they make rapid solid progress onto their objectives.

8 1600hrs: realizing that 33rd Brigade's absence is creating a yawning gap in the advance, 13th Australian Brigade's left-hand battalion (52nd) shifts their axis left, inadvertently exacerbating the hole created by failure in Blauwepoortbeek Valley. 33rd Brigade arrives at 1630hrs and exploits beyond the Australians to capture Van Hove and Joye Farms.

9 1730hrs: a mixed counterattack by 1st Guards Reserve and 5th Bavarian Regiments is repulsed on Hun's Walk but the SOS barrage lands on Australian troops, triggering a chaotic wholesale withdrawal back to the Black Line. Only 52nd Battalion on Wambeek manages to reoccupy gains immediately.

10 1900hrs: after a four-and-a-half hour afternoon preparatory bombardment, 142nd Brigade has another go at Spoil Bank. Their attacking battalion (40th) is repulsed with 30 per cent casualties. No further attempts are made on 7 June.

THE BATTLE OF MESSINES RIDGE

7 June 1917, British Second Army phase two advances viewed from the South, 0900hrs to 1900hrs; plus German counterattacks

The Blauwepoortbeek Valley looking west towards 4th Australian Division's avenue of attack. The Oosttaverne Line was thicker in the south and shielded by a chequerboard of pillboxes. (Author's collection)

The Australian Official History blends the recollections of men present during those final moments before attack: '… the aeroplanes wheeling, fighting in the brilliant sky; the German shells punching roan coloured dust plumes from the ruins on the summit; tanks marshalling in the meadows; batteries of [horse-drawn] artillery racing up through the long grass, unlimbering, the teams trotting back with a jangle of chains.'[36]

At 1510hrs precisely, the creeping barrage opened up once more. The 4th Australian Division had the most work to do; the Oosttaverne Line was thicker and more confused astride the river Douve than elsewhere. Being a natural thoroughfare for German traffic up onto Messines Ridge, the Douve Valley had become a maze of communication trenches that ran alongside overgrown hedgerows. This sector also had a second line with trenches that were uncompleted in many areas, vexing commanders of supporting companies tasked with their capture. Worst of all, objectives were picketed by a belt of stout pillboxes that thus far had avoided protracted barrage.

Whether by accident or design, Plumer could not have picked a better body of men to tackle this challenge. Recent veterans of the gruelling Bullecourt front at Arras, these troops were among the hardest and most committed in BEF – primed by an aggravating afternoon of German shelling.

The southern axis was covered by 12th Brigade, stretching from Blauwepoortbeek down to the river Douve. Their assaulting battalions enjoyed the assistance of three tanks (one of which was imaginatively self-titled 'Rumblebelly') and soon overran 'Oxygen Trench', an outlying bulwark. Yet already fire intensified, chiefly from the pillboxes straddling 'Hun's Walk' – the Messines to Warneton road.

Casualties mounted, especially among junior officers maintaining the advance through example. However, attacking platoons were able to apply their well-rehearsed template for strongpoint destruction depicted in the battlescene illustration on pp. 76–77. This involved peppering the firing apertures with a Lewis Gun and then working bombing parties around to the vulnerable flanks and rear entrance of the pillbox. Defensive planners precluded such a manoeuvre by siting pillboxes in view of mutually supporting trenches; in this case the creeping barrage had screened them off.

36. *Official History of Australia in the War of 1914–1918*, C. E. W. Bean, 1929

Nonetheless, even taken piecemeal, the pillboxes demanded singular aggression – and a ruthlessness that permeates all contemporary accounts. Bunkers are inhuman objects; the pitiless reach of their machine guns unimaginably malevolent. Courageous men – close friends – spring forwards only to be pummelled and disfigured into a lifeless heap with audible ferocity: a spectacle that can drain courage as readily as pulling a plug from a sink. But of course there are souls behind the bunker's vindictive black eye, deafened by the report of their weapon, gagging on propellant fumes sharp like the ammonia from animal urine, and fumbling with shaking hands to free fresh ammunition belts.

The conclusions exposed feral extremes of violence. If they don't kill in the confines of a pillbox, grenades will concuss, gifting a vital few seconds to the assaulting infantrymen. Private Wilfred Gallwey of 47th Battalion cleared one of these pillboxes on 7 June:

> The gun in this blockhouse was now silenced.... [We] walked right up the place and a couple of men went to the entrance where the gun crew was found all huddled up inside. No time was lost here however and [our]... men fired point blank into the group. There was a noise as though pigs were being killed. They squealed and made guttural noises which gave place to groans after which all was silent. The bodies were all thrown in a heap outside the block house to make sure all were dead.... It was a good thing this hornet's nest had been cleaned out so easily. Nearly all were young men.
> *Diary of Private Wilfred D Gallwey, held by the Australian War Memorial – Record 3DRL/0361*

There is no such thing as 'civilized' warfare. Callous as Private Gallwey sounds, his unit had often been fired at from behind by wounded men they spared.

One of the numerous German bunkers on the Oosttaverne Line. This shows the rear entrance that assaulting platoons would try and work around towards. Shattered terrain and the warren of surrounding communications trenches actually aided the task. (IWM Q 2310)

PILLBOX FIGHTING – CAPTURE OF THE OOSTTAVERNE LINE, 7 JUNE 1917 (pp. 76–77)

The 37th Australian Battalion was on temporary attachment to 12th Brigade, 4th Australian Division, for the final phase of Second Army's Messines Ridge operation: the advance to the Oosttaverne Line, a belt of defences that formed the 'bowstring' behind Gruppe Wytschaete's bulging Messines Salient. The ANZACs were responsible for the southern half of the offensive's frontage in the low ground beyond the village of Messines itself. The defences were picketed by concrete bunkers (pillboxes) in a mutually supporting chequerboard. Of stout breezeblock construction and protected by belts of wire, these pillboxes presented a serious proposition for assaulting infantry with only limited tank support. Three were operating to the north of the 4th Australian Division's axis **(1)** but not in a position to influence events for the 37th Battalion. With the creeping barrage isolating pillboxes from depth defences, platoons captured them piecemeal utilizing a basic combination of suppression and flanking manoeuvre. These 'fire and movement' tactics had been adopted across the BEF and were proving highly effective. Rifle bombers and the Lewis Gun team positioned themselves with good arcs onto the pillbox's primary orientation **(2)** while the 'bomber' section worked around to a position where they could approach unseen and get grenades through the firing slits. This portion of the Osttaverne Line was manned by the 18th Bavarian Infantry Regiment, who had come forwards as reinforcements that morning. They have attempted to counter flanking tactics by posting a Maxim 08/15 in the

blind side sap **(3)**. Despite inflicting two casualties **(4)**, it has been overcome and the bombers have successfully posted their grenades, leaving the telltale sooty pall of smoke emanating from the pillbox's firing slits and entrance. Fleeing survivors are being cut down and the assault party is closing in to clear the interior. It was a grim business, quarter very seldom being given. Ignoring the entreaties of one terrified Bavarian, the lead bomber readies his bayonet thrust **(5)**. The Australian Official History is eloquent on the nature of this combat:

*Temporarily half mad, their pulses pounding at their ears…
the less self controlled are for the time being governed by reckless,
primitive impulse. With death singing about their ears, they will kill
until they grow tired of killing. The routing out of enemy troops
from behind several feet of concrete is almost inevitably the signal
for a butchery of at least the first few who emerge.… It is idle for the
reader to cry shame on such incidents for this frenzy is an inevitable
condition in desperate fighting. Ruthlessness is a quality essential in
hand-to-hand fighting.*

The Australians were tenacious troops and well suited to the environment. They made good progress that afternoon, albeit at a particularly high cost to officers and non-commissioned officers at the fore. One other friction-causing delay was their propensity for looting corpses – something one soldier is being upbraided for here **(6)**.

37th Battalion from 3rd Australian Division had an independent axis at the extreme south of phase two's advance. They too struck the pillbox line. Captain Bob Grieve saw his company decimated; all of the platoon commanders were casualties. Grabbing a satchel of grenades, he ran forwards himself, covering the advance by landing bombs in the pillbox's field of fire. Once flat against it, he then killed the occupants with two grenades posted through the aperture.

After these redoubts had been vanquished, the battalions were soon into the Oosttaverne Line proper and much of its garrison fled in preference to a brawl with the Australians. Distinctions between 'leading' and 'supporting' companies were now blurred by casualty rates so the planned leapfrog gave way to a more spontaneous and pragmatic bound onto the incomplete second line; communications trenches and scrub patches being cleaned out in like fashion.

Blauwepoortbeek Valley was split between 12th Brigade and their neighbours, the 13th, to the north. In military operations, crests make better unit boundaries than the base of defiles because any attack up or down a valley will demand coordinated fire support across it. Even so, it is unlikely that a homogeneous force would have made headway: defences had been augmented by survivors from 1st Guard Reserve Regiment's lunchtime counterattack and were sited to maximize the defensive qualities of gullies that channelled any easterly advance. Moreover, wire here was in good condition. Each Australian brigade had one battalion in the valley (45th and 49th respectively) and they shared the same fate: within a few hundred metres some attacking companies had lost all officers and sergeants; every single company commander in 49th Battalion was killed. The Bavarians had field artillery in this area able to pour direct fire into the assault from 300m (1,000ft); owing to their reliance on concrete emplacements, the creeping barrage had passed over ineffectually for once.

A view of Blauwepoortbeek Valley in 1917. Though taken later in the year, the photograph is worthy of comparison with the image on p. 74. Shellfire had 'ploughed' the ground, destroying much of the vegetation. However, the flooding seen here was not evident in June, which was largely dry. (IWM E 1364)

Given the concentration of force achieved across Messines Ridge on 7 June, the exploits of 13th Brigade's other battalion (52nd) will come as a surprise. They were attacking up the Wambeek Valley to the north, supposedly shared with IX Corps' sole attacking brigade, the 33rd (from 11th Division). As has been explained, there were delays and the British were nowhere to be seen. Recognizing that resistance was slight in this valley, an enterprising 52nd Battalion company commander pushed left, stretching his frontage to incorporate the absent ally's objectives. Though dangerously tenuous, the risk paid off; when a 33rd Brigade battalion arrived at 1630hrs, they were able to exploit beyond the Australians and capture Joye and Van Hove farms, from which snipers had harassed 52nd Battalion's consolidation efforts.

However, their oblique shift had pulled the rest of 13th Brigade in the same direction, exacerbating the gap created by failure in Blauwepoortbeek Valley; the upshot being a kilometre-wide gap in the 4th Division's front line when they went firm on the Oosttaverne Line that afternoon.

The 57th Brigade (borrowed from 19th Division) covered the other half of 33rd Brigade's frontage. Here they learned the value of simplicity in planning; all that was asked of the companies was to advance in a given direction following a creeping barrage. They knew the ridge well from models. It was remarkably straightforward through the village of Oosttaverne – seized 20 minutes into phase two.

X Corps' two attacking brigades also had a joyfully humdrum advance to the Oosttaverne Line. The two lead battalions of 17th Brigade sustained *only six casualties* between them. Only on the left, where the other brigade (73rd) shared a boundary with the 47th Division, was there any complication: Spoil Bank remained in enemy hands so the line necessitated adjustment in order to ensure integrity come nightfall. The 142nd Brigade had another go at Spoil Bank in the early evening following a four-hour heavy artillery bombardment. Again it failed; German machine guns had survived intact.

II ANZAC operations, 8–11 June

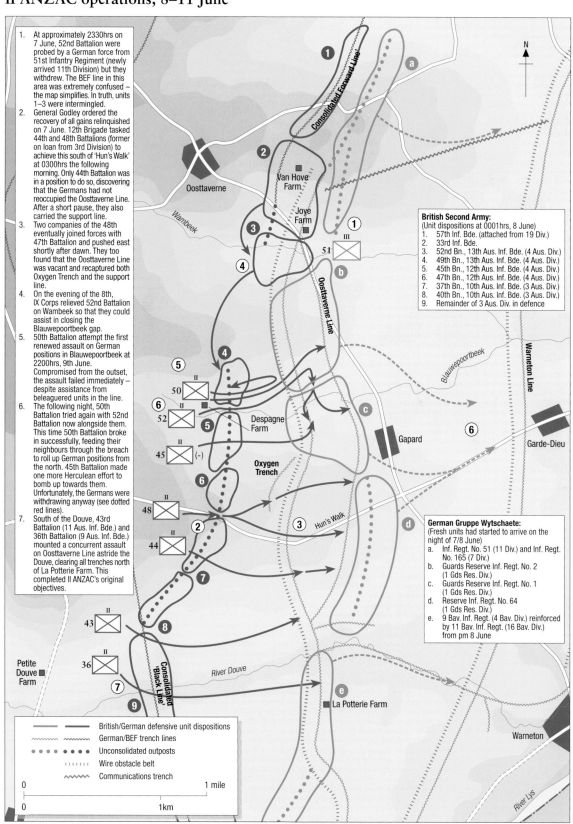

1. At approximately 2330hrs on 7 June, 52nd Battalion were probed by a German force from 51st Infantry Regiment (newly arrived 11th Division) but they withdrew. The BEF line in this area was extremely confused – the map simplifies. In truth, units 1–3 were intermingled.

2. General Godley ordered the recovery of all gains relinquished on 7 June. 12th Brigade tasked 44th and 48th Battalions (former on loan from 3rd Division) to achieve this south of 'Hun's Walk' at 0300hrs the following morning. Only 44th Battalion was in a position to do so, discovering that the Germans had not reoccupied the Oosttaverne Line. After a short pause, they also carried the support line.

3. Two companies of the 48th eventually joined forces with 47th Battalion and pushed east shortly after dawn. They too found that the Oosttaverne Line was vacant and recaptured both Oxygen Trench and the support line.

4. On the evening of the 8th, IX Corps relieved 52nd Battalion on Wambeek so that they could assist in closing the Blauwepoortbeek gap.

5. 50th Battalion attempt the first renewed assault on German positions in Blauwepoortbeek at 2200hrs, 9th June. Compromised from the outset, the assault failed immediately – despite assistance from beleaguered units in the line.

6. The following night, 50th Battalion tried again with 52nd Battalion now alongside them. This time 50th Battalion broke in successfully, feeding their neighbours through the breach to roll up German positions from the north. 45th Battalion made one more Herculean effort to bomb up towards them. Unfortunately, the Germans were withdrawing anyway (see dotted red lines).

7. South of the Douve, 43rd Battalion (11 Aus. Inf. Bde.) and 36th Battalion (9 Aus. Inf. Bde.) mounted a concurrent assault on Oosttaverne Line astride the Douve, clearing all trenches north of La Potterie Farm. This completed II ANZAC's original objectives.

British Second Army:
(Unit dispositions at 0001hrs, 8 June)
1. 57th Inf. Bde. (attached from 19 Div.)
2. 33rd Inf. Bde.
3. 52nd Bn., 13th Aus. Inf. Bde. (4 Aus. Div.)
4. 49th Bn., 13th Aus. Inf. Bde. (4 Aus. Div.)
5. 45th Bn., 12th Aus. Inf. Bde. (4 Aus. Div.)
6. 47th Bn., 12th Aus. Inf. Bde. (4 Aus. Div.)
7. 37th Bn., 10th Aus. Inf. Bde. (3 Aus. Div.)
8. 40th Bn., 10th Aus. Inf. Bde. (3 Aus. Div.)
9. Remainder of 3 Aus. Div. in defence

German Gruppe Wytschaete:
(Fresh units had started to arrive on the night of 7/8 June)
a. Inf. Regt. No. 51 (11 Div.) and Inf. Regt. No. 165 (7 Div.)
b. Guards Reserve Inf. Regt. No. 2 (1 Gds Res. Div.)
c. Guards Reserve Inf. Regt. No. 1 (1 Gds Res. Div.)
d. Reserve Inf. Regt. No. 64 (1 Gds Res. Div.)
e. 9 Bav. Inf. Regt. (4 Bav. Div.) reinforced by 11 Bav. Inf. Regt. (16 Bav. Div.) from pm 8 June

Oosttaverne
Van Hove Farm
Joye Farm
Wambeek
Blauwepoortbeek
Warneton Line
Despagne Farm
Gapard
Garde-Dieu
Oxygen Trench
Hun's Walk
Petite Douve Farm
Consolidated 'Black Line'
River Douve
La Potterie Farm
Warneton
River Lys

Legend:
- British/German defensive unit dispositions
- German/BEF trench lines
- Unconsolidated outposts
- Wire obstacle belt
- Communications trench

0 ——— 1 mile
0 ——— 1km

British troops recover a German 7.7cm field gun from Messines Ridge. The final tally of captured artillery pieces disappointed Second Army but many of the gun positions west of the Oosttaverne Line had been evacuated. (IWM Q 5480)

That aside, the marked difference in character between north and south axes during phase two seems difficult to fathom. It is best explained by three factors. First, the topography of Blauwepoortbeek and Douve valleys are more suited to defence; there are shallow folds and gullies not immediately obvious on a map. The line was thicker there with a higher proportion of concrete emplacements; and finally, it had received more reinforcements during the day.

Recall also that German commanders planned to rely heavily on artillery in their defence of Messines Ridge. Second Army planners had expected to capture as many as 120 German artillery pieces on the slopes above the Oosttaverne Line. Many limbered up and fled during the five-hour pause; others stayed as long as possible before abandoning the guns and extracting on foot. One German artilleryman with 1st Field Artillery Regiment (in 2nd Division's rear area) recalls their flight: 'We had a terrible job getting back through the enemy curtain of fire. I dragged and carried a wounded infantryman, who had lost both eyes due to a shell splinter. He kept begging me to shoot him. It was simply dreadful.'[37]

In the end just 48 guns were found – and most of them had been damaged by counterbattery fire.

NOT SO FRIENDLY FIRE

As the British artillery barrage dissipated, harassing fire from German snipers and machine guns beyond the Oosttaverne Line flared up. Worst affected were the disparate positions of Australian 12th Brigade attempting to dig in astride Hun's Walk – inadvertently further forwards than planned. Sensing their isolation, a mixed force from Germany's 1st Guards Reserve and 5th Bavarian Infantry Regiments counterattacked at 1730hrs. Hastily the Australian officers organized a firing line along a hedgerow, meeting the attackers with an intense fusillade. By all accounts, the men stood up to achieve better fields of fire – Lee-Enfield barrels overheated and one enormous soldier fired his Lewis Gun from the shoulder.

37. *History of Field Artillery Regiment 1*, Oberstleutnant Alfred Laeger, 1939 – translated by Col. Jack Sheldon

Signalling for artillery support, the Australians suddenly found themselves under intense bombardment. Their guns were registered onto preplanned grids. Instead of creating a protective curtain, the shells rained onto friendly forces. With no way to communicate their predicament, someone ordered a retirement. Thinking they were missing something, neighbouring commanders did likewise. Confusion spread. Seeing withdrawing troops arrive at their backstop position on the Black Line, staff officers from the New Zealand Division brought defensive barrage coordinates back to the Oosttaverne Line, shelling those units (such as the 37th Battalion) that had remained. Rumours of widespread German counterattacks abounded. By 2200hrs, less 52nd Battalion on the extreme left, the entire II ANZAC front had withdrawn to the Black Line, surrendering gains made that afternoon.

Arrival of German reinforcements opposite IX Corps was interpreted similarly. Here too the artillery fired short (also later at the behest of staffs believing there had been a general retirement). Fortunately, order was restored – and forward positions reoccupied – before wholesale withdrawal could solidify.

Inherent limitations in command and control came home to roost again that night, probably coloured by Plumer's caution: when in doubt, battlefield commanders (i.e. brigade and below) defaulted to the Black Line. As soon as the news reached II ANZAC's commander, Lieutenant-General Godley, he ordered the 3rd and 4th Australian Divisions to retake the Oosttaverne Line without delay.

TAKE TWO

Having suffered his fair share of confusion that day, Laffert was finally getting to grips with Gruppe Wytschaete's predicament. The failure of the afternoon counterattacks disavowed him of any notion that Messines Ridge could be recovered. Indeed, intuitively he favoured a withdrawal east of Ypres–Comines Canal. When it became apparent that the British were consolidating he reneged, ordering instead that his *Feldgrauen* hold existing dispositions. There is ample evidence that German senior officers (and even reinforcing battalion commanders unfamiliar with the ground) still believed the entire Oosttaverne Line to be in German hands. In reality, their forward lines were, in places, merely sections spread out along shell holes. The 7th Infantry Division had finally arrived in full. One of its battalions (from the 165th Infantry Regiment) probed towards Australian positions north of Wambeek in the early evening but theirs was now a defensive mission. Earlier Gruppe Ypres had released the 11th Infantry Division and they dribbled in throughout the night, filling in the centre. At this stage, the Warneton Line was Laffert's insurance.

The ANZACs did not give them too long to settle in. Their first attack came at 0300hrs between 'Hun's Walk' and the river Douve using two fresh battalions (44th and 48th) bolstered by the indefatigable remnants of the 47th and 45th Battalions – now either marching, digging or in action for over 24 hours. They felt their way forwards using scouts to check whether positions were occupied, discovering that Germans had not taken advantage of the Australians' temporary retirement. Only desultory long-range machine-gun fire met their advance. The 47th Battalion even found a Lewis Gun team that had opted to remain in position.

LEFT
Australian infantry in hastily prepared forward positions. Although this photograph was taken later in the Third Ypres offensive, it illustrates the kind of dispositions that they were clinging to – and evacuated – on the evening of 7 June. (IWM E 774)

RIGHT
Plumer revised his scheme for solidifying the new British front line; planned culminations were not as commanding as he had hoped. These soldiers are consulting a trench map in a captured German communications trench on Messines Ridge. They were scheduled to advance again on 14 June. (IWM Q 2314)

In the Blauwepoortbeek Valley, the 49th Battalion had also been ordered to advance in concert but they were far too exhausted and depleted to comply. On hearing this, the 4th Australian Division's commander, Major-General Holmes, telephoned his brigadiers. They knew nothing. 'Well now; it seems the only way is for us to go up and see. Get your hats and come along'[38] His personal reconnaissance revealed the true extent of the 52nd Battalion's overstretch so it was agreed that IX Corps would assume responsibility for that part of the line from last light on 8 June, freeing the 52nd to assist their neighbours in clearing Blauwepoortbeek.

8 June was another fine and hot day. It passed quietly for everyone except the 3rd Australian Division, who suffered a hurricane barrage after German airmen spied their trench construction programme. The relief of the 52nd Battalion triggered yet another panicked response from artillery observers, inflicting significant casualties on both formations involved and imposing delay on the Blauwepoortbeek operation. The exasperating regularity of this occurrence betrays a rare flaw in Plumer's planning – the original divisions consolidated on Black Line had insufficient liaison with phase two divisions now clinging to the Oosttaverne Line. Today this would be easier to address; when applied to Great War communications it was a recipe for the chaos that ensued.

The situation was rectified only when Second Army reorganized the defence of Messines Ridge on 9 June. Immediately upon reaching the Oosttaverne Line two days previously, it was apparent that the southern end was not as commanding as they had hoped. II ANZAC's commander, Godley, concurred. A scheme was hatched whereby Second Army would extend their advance on 14 June and construct fresh positions further down the convex slope. Reorganization was the first step. Henceforth, divisions would be allocated a portion of line in depth, the Oosttaverne Line forming the front, with the 'main defensive position' where Black Line was.

38. Quoted in *Official History of Australia in the War of 1914–1918*, C. E. W. Bean, 1929

II ANZAC was thus able to put the New Zealand Division into reserve; IX Corps did the same with the 36th and 16th Divisions. Bear in mind how long troops had now been committed: marching all day on the 6 June, fighting through the 7th and digging trenches on the 8th and 9th. Diaries attest to men planting a shovel in the ground, falling asleep, and then being woken by comrades to lift it out. Sentries hallucinate at this stage – possibly another explanation for jittery artillery observation.

The ANZACs still had fighting to do. Most histories place the next Australian attempt to close Blauwepoortbeek at 2200hrs on 10 June. In fact there was an identical operation by the 50th Battalion 24 hours earlier. It failed owing to early detection of the advance, which then blundered into unbroken wire. The 45th Battalion – by now 'desperately weary' – attempted to support them. Indeed, one company had spent all afternoon in a bombing duel over a pillbox.

After another personal reconnaissance, Holmes requested a day-long barrage and added a second battalion (52nd). The 10 June night attack fared better. Once the 50th Battalion broke in, other companies from the 52nd (which had failed on a frontal assault) were fed through to bomb along the German positions. Such a brief paragraph does no justice to the tenacity of Australian troops that night: incredibly, the 45th put in yet another assault on the flanks.

One hour later, the 3rd Australian Division mounted a similar successful advance south of Hun's Walk up the Douve Valley with two battalions, though excessive barrel wear on their gun-lines led to more costly erratic shooting.

Unbeknownst to them at the time, II ANZAC's operation was unnecessary. On 9 June, Armin met Army Group North Commander, Kronprinz Rupprecht. They decided to withdraw from the area – even the Warneton Line was deemed inappropriate: obsolete and lacking vantage points for artillery observation. Necessary improvements to the Flandern Stellung 5km (3 miles) rearwards would take a fortnight so they ordered Laffert to hold an improvised intermediary position between Houthem and Warneton. If this was not attacked during that timeframe, they would consider occupying it permanently. By now all of Gruppe Wytschaete's original divisions had been relieved.

Prisoners captured by the Australians on 10 June disclosed that they were in the midst of this withdrawal when attacked. With phase two objectives finally consolidated and Gruppe Wytschaete on the march, Plumer brought forwards his timetable for tertiary advance by 48 hours to the night of 11–12 June. The vacuum was filled without significant incident. Spoil Bank, which was to be the northern anchor, capitulated. By 14 June, Second Army had tidied the line and established all outposts, bringing their offensive to a close.

AFTERMATH

THE ZENITH OF SIEGE WARFARE

At teatime on 7 June, Haig visited Plumer to congratulate him. Warm words were exchanged. That evening, Haig described Plumer as 'his most reliable Army Commander'[39] and commented in his diary that 'the old man deserves the highest praise'.[40] Messines Ridge was a stunning achievement: so much gained at such little cost. Spirits soared during those early stages. Yet, all too soon, little tensions resurfaced. They tarnish the historiography of Messines to this day. Why was that momentum not exploited? Similar questions are levelled at the conspicuous operational successes of Vimy Ridge and Cambrai in the same year. With so much more slaughter on the horizon, it is frustrating to consider lost opportunities.

Messines Ridge always carried limited objectives; favoured axis for breakthrough was further north. The debate throughout conception centred on its interrelation with parallel operational aims. Only after it was divorced from the northern aspect of Third Ypres in early May did exploitation become an issue; before that, attacks would be taking place elsewhere anyway. Haig broached the issue with Plumer on 24 May, stressing that 'reserves will be placed at the disposal of General Gough… in order to enable him to cooperate in an effort to gain [Passchendaele Ridge]'.[41] Plumer was enthusiastic, replying in the affirmative on 3 June. He favoured an attack with two corps (II and VIII) along the Menin Road.

Note however that this correspondence is taking place within a fortnight of Zero Hour. Haig spoke to Gough again on the eve of battle and there was still discussion over who would command any follow-on offensive. Discourse occupied the margins and it seems like a half-hearted contingency, perhaps because there were good reasons for a distinct pause before attempting attack elsewhere – chiefly reallocation of artillery.

The matter arose again on 8 June. Clearly buoyed by the previous day's fortunes, Haig asked Plumer how soon he could drive on his subsidiary axis: 72 hours. Second Army needed to transfer 60 heavy and medium guns. Again, one must ask how serious they were about this. Three corps had just attacked with 756 guns of this calibre; now two were supposed to do the same with an uplift of 60. Gough – supposedly the more aggressive of the two army

39. Comment recorded by Brig. Gen. John Charteris, BEF Chief of Intelligence, in his memoir At GHQ, 1931
40. Diary entry 7 June, Haig Papers, National Library of Scotland
41. Quoted in British Official History, *Messines and Third Ypres 1917*, Brig. Gen. Sir James Edmonds, 1948

commanders – was given the lead but after deliberating (for six days) he expressed caution. The attack would create a vulnerable salient; better to stick to the plan set on 7 May. Having received reports that German forces had pushed reserves into the Gheluvelt area, Haig concurred. Plumer's apologists vindicate him at this juncture, claiming that it was Haig and Gough that got cold feet.

It is more illuminating to take a step back from the specifics of these rivalries and examine the feasibility of any exploitation – planned or otherwise. Generally, the prime sources of frustration among historians are the German staff dispatches expressing terror that their defences were wide open, hence opportunity. However, you need capability to snatch opportunity. Second Army's entire operation was focused on seizing and consolidating set objectives. To achieve this, they deliberately shelled and cratered the entire frontage, rendering it impassable to all but man, pack animal and tank. The concentration of force necessary to ensure survival of their infantry consumed 40 per cent of the entire BEF's heavy artillery on a 15km (9-mile) frontage. This was not a nimble beast. Recall also the uncertainties prevalent at dusk on 7 June and then the sacrifices of II ANZAC; Plumer's sacrosanct objectives were not fully met until midnight on the 10th.

Oft quoted in relation to Messines is the British military historian Sir Basil Liddell Hart: 'The capture of Messines Ridge by Plumer's Second Army was almost the only true siege-warfare attack made throughout a siege war. It was also one of the few attacks until late 1918 in which the methods employed... fitted the facts of the situation.'[42]

Irishmen of the 16th Division withdraw from Messines Ridge to rest areas after the battle. One hopes they got the opportunity to escape for a few hours in the arms of cheap whisky and song. Note the souvenir *Pickelhaube* sported by one of the men on the tailgate. (IWM Q 4198)

42. *History of the First World War*, Sir Basil Liddell Hart, 1970

This is a more constructive start point for understanding the significance of Messines. Plumer understood the limitations on manoeuvre better than most – and it was this conceptual grasp that laid the foundations for Second Army's emphatic victory.

Above all else, Plumer applied a patient strategy; he understood there would be no cheap wins in this war. Furthermore, he spoke the language of military operations. Logistics, thorough administration and detailed staff work were at the heart of Second Army's preparations – then followed through with meticulous training. Naturally there were shortfalls such as the consistent confusion over defensive artillery barrages. Inherent limitations in battlefield communications must bear their share of the blame. Plumer innovated to overcome this technology lag; for example, his reliance on gifted young liaison officers over formal subordinate situation reports was later copied by Field Marshal Montgomery, then serving as a staff officer in IX Corps.

Harnessing the vision of John Norton-Griffiths and his coterie was Plumer's way of turning these realities to best advantage; mines are the epitome of siege warfare. Their application as a springboard for an offensive of this size involved risk (luck played its part in keeping the scheme secret) but paid off. Unquestionably, the mines won Second Army their initial objectives and arguably unhinged Gruppe Wytschaete's entire forward-area defensive plan.

Nonetheless, there was much more to Messines than mines. Plumer reached into the future of warfare as well as its past. Air power opened up dead ground to target acquisition, aided battlefield situational awareness through 'contact patrols' and delivered ordnance deep behind enemy lines.

Then there was artillery – king of the Great War. One cannot overemphasize the part played by artillery in Second Army's successes. Plumer's guns formed the backbone of his entire offensive, through both preparation and execution. His staff mastered and employed the very latest techniques in counterbattery practice, thereby neutralizing the gravest threat to assaulting infantry. Sometimes overlooked is artillery's cumulative effect on German morale. Assailed for two weeks prior to 7 June, it is possible that the mines simply toppled a rotten edifice. Yet in the guise employed at Messines, artillery was almost as much a siege weapon as the mines; look no further than the railway lines to heavy gun positions.

Final front-line positions at Messines and the Third Ypres offensive in outline

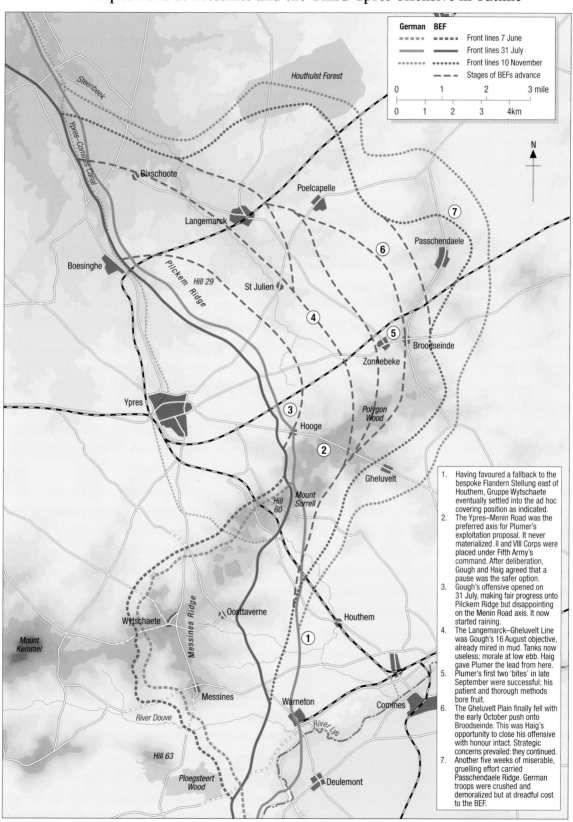

German | BEF

- ---- / ---- Front lines 7 June
- ──── / ──── Front lines 31 July
- ····· / ····· Front lines 10 November
- ─ ─ ─ Stages of BEFs advance

| 0 | 1 | 2 | 3 mile |
| 0 | 1 | 2 | 3 | 4km |

Houthulst Forest

Steenbeek

Ypres-Comines Canal

Bixschoote

Poelcapelle

Langemarck

⑦

Passchendaele

Boesinghe

Pilckem Ridge

Hill 29

St Julien

④

⑥

Broodseinde

⑤

Zonnebeke

Ypres

③

Hooge

Polygon Wood

②

Gheluvelt

Hill 60

Mount Sorrell

Mount Kemmel

Wytschaete

Messines Ridge

Oosttaverne

Houthem

①

Comines

Messines

Warneton

River Douve

River Lys

Hill 63

Ploegsteert Wood

Deulemont

1. Having favoured a fallback to the bespoke Flandern Stellung east of Houthem, Gruppe Wytschaete eventually settled into the ad hoc covering position as indicated.
2. The Ypres–Menin Road was the preferred axis for Plumer's exploitation proposal. It never materialized. II and VIII Corps were placed under Fifth Army's command. After deliberation, Gough and Haig agreed that a pause was the safer option.
3. Gough's offensive opened on 31 July, making fair progress onto Pilckem Ridge but disappointing on the Menin Road axis. It now started raining.
4. The Langemarck–Gheluvelt Line was Gough's 16 August objective, already mired in mud. Tanks now useless; morale at low ebb. Haig gave Plumer the lead from here.
5. Plumer's first two 'bites' in late September were successful; his patient and thorough methods bore fruit.
6. The Gheluvelt Plain finally fell with the early October push onto Broodseinde. This was Haig's opportunity to close his offensive with honour intact. Strategic concerns prevailed: they continued.
7. Another five weeks of miserable, gruelling effort carried Passchendaele Ridge. German troops were crushed and demoralized but at dreadful cost to the BEF.

Messines was a product of its time, all too evanescent. A mining scheme on that scale was unrepeatable. Messines had been the tunneller's *magnum opus*. Thereafter they spent an increasing proportion of their time dedicated to subway and dugout construction. From now on, precocious technologies like the tank were ascendant. Being basic and cumbersome, they were still no silver bullet. But this is where a battle like Messines had a unique vantage point. As the zenith of one way of war, it could spy the path to another.

Unfortunately, the jaws of constraint were not ready to relax their grip on Great War commanders. Third Ypres scarred particularly badly.

PASSCHENDAELE

The Germans knew what was coming. Army Group North's Chief of Staff, General von Kuhl, later wrote: 'There was complete clarity on the German side that a major British offensive in Flanders was to be expected.... What was completely uncertain, however, was when it was due to begin. It was obvious that the British had imposed an operational pause [after Messines].'[43]

Their own recriminations were swift. General von Laffert was blamed for gross misuse of his *Eingreif* divisions and removed from command within a week. Apparently, he should not have committed his trained divisions to the line and brought in units unfamiliar with the area. It is difficult to see what choice he had with the resources available – especially since Army Group North refused to thin down the Arras front until it became patently obvious that Messines was under imminent attack. Sadly, we do not know enough about their reasoning to make a full judgement. Laffert died of a heart attack the following July.

Attention then turned onto Füsslein's assessments of British mining. One can find quotes from Füsslein to support any hypothesis; the key observation is that he vacillated, which indicates that he probably just did not know. After the event, Füsslein levelled some reasonable accusations at German High Command over lack of focus and resources. In truth – brave as his *Pioniere* undoubtedly were – the British simply outmined them.

Had Füsslein phrased strong and unequivocal warnings, it may have swung the debate about whether to cede Messines Ridge willingly. Relinquishing such a key feature is much easier said than done. Hence one should be suspicious of men like Kuhl being wise after the event. The fact is that both Rupprecht and Armin deferred to the opinions of Laffert and Gruppe Wytschaete's divisional commanders. Rather than assuming responsibility for a decision they presided over, it appears Laffert was sacrificed. But the German Army learnt from the experience of Messines and commissioned an inquiry into their failures. Besides obvious points like the effect of mines and counterbattery fire, it cited useful lessons on the imprudence of cramped forward slope dispositions. These were applied to defensive preparations at Ypres.

The BEF's offensive was scheduled to commence on 31 July. A compromise on the Messines exploitation debate might be to ask whether or not Haig could have done more to fulfil his 7 May pledge to 'wear down and exhaust the enemy's resistance' by advancing Third Ypres' timetable. This at least would have made the most of fair weather. Regrettably for his infantry, the intervening period was dominated by high-level political debates about the validity of the entire enterprise – also probably inescapable.

43. *Der Weltkrieg 1914–18*, Gen. Hermann von Kuhl, 1929 – translated by Col. Jack Sheldon

Gough's Fifth Army offensive opened as planned, just in time for protracted rain. The subsequent fortunes of Third Ypres warrant at least one Campaign title, possibly more. Suffice it to say that progress was made towards Pilckem Ridge, just not on the key central axis along Menin Road (where Plumer had entertained the idea of a subsidiary offensive in June).

Relentless downpours negated the value of tanks and created delay in the next phase, which opened on 16 August. As is well documented, shelling had destroyed the drainage system. Troops moving into assembly areas did so along duckboard paths. Gough's second push sought to dislodge Armin from the line at Langemarck. It ground to a halt after two days.

Haig grew impatient with Gough (reflecting the mood of miserable infantrymen) and switched command of the offensive to Plumer – something of a poisoned chalice by now. True to form, Plumer did his best. In the first instance he argued for a pause while he planned deliberate 'bite and hold' operations employing overwhelming artillery bombardment and concentration of force. The first of these was directed along the Menin Road on 20 September, followed swiftly by another at Polygon Wood on the 26th. Both battles followed the same pattern: rapid gains consolidated in time to crush the *Eingreif* formations. They caused a crisis of confidence among German commanders who then questioned the practice of thinning out front lines. This led to higher casualties later in the battle. Gheluvelt Plain finally fell on 4 October.

German fortunes were then saved by the weather, which broke again in earnest. Tactically, Haig had every excuse to cease the offensive at this point but elected not to do so, citing the (debatable) support of his army commanders and a plethora of strategic concerns: support to ailing France, deception to conceal Allied offensive operations in Italy and maintaining pressure on Germany after Russian capitulation.

So they toiled on through the battle of Poelcappelle (9 October) and the now-infamous battles for Passchendaele from 12 October to 10 November. Detail is unnecessary: territorial gains were limited and disproportionate to the cost. But the *Feldgrauen* shivering and dying in their shell holes suffered grievously.

In the context of an attritional struggle with American troops en route, Germany was under much more pressure. Meaningless as this may seem in the context of British losses almost unfathomable today, on a coldly detached academic level it was relevant to the eventual outcome of the Great War. Any contemporary judgement on the value of that sacrifice is inherently subjective. It was that unfortunate generation's cross to bear.

For all Plumer's careful increments during Third Ypres – of which Messines was the first and most conspicuous – it finished back where it started at the close of 1916, with comparative tallies of hideous casualty figures. Many argue that it would have been different had he been given consistent stewardship; this is probably true. Yet there is also a sense that the parameters were simply beyond his control.

THE BATTLEFIELD TODAY

With its gothic buildings and ramparts, Ypres has an apt character to receive so many British pilgrims every year. On a summer's weekend, the broad town square is thronged; terraced bars give refuge to slightly exhausted-looking families and groups of burly men debating the merits of Gough's generalship over tall glasses of lager. North-west Flanders is definitely one corner of a foreign field that will forever be England. Visitors will find English-language bookshops and pubs seemingly kidnapped from middle England. In Ploegsteert, there is even an incongruous hostelry called 'The Australian'.

Messines Ridge lies so close to the city limits that a bicycle excursion is feasible. All but the most cursory exploration will benefit from the 1:50,000 IGN map of Ypres (27-28-36). Peter Oldham's 'Battleground Europe' guidebook entitled *Messines Ridge* is also a great help. Unlike so many Great War features flattered by the term 'hill' or 'ridge', the significance of Messines is immediately apparent. Many aspects of my narrative will leap to life: the nakedness of German front-line positions, convex eastern slopes and Blauwepoortbeek Valley's natural defensive configuration.

Hill 63 affords particularly good views of the 3rd Australian Division's initial objectives and is a quiet spot to sit and imagine the awe-inspiring mine blasts of Zero Hour. Most of the mine craters are still in evidence. Indeed, one of the few to be filled in was the abandoned Birdcage III that detonated in 1955 when struck by lightning. They are tranquil ponds now, frequented by anglers and picnickers. Spanbroekmolen crater has been retitled 'Pool of Peace' and bears a modest memorial.

Spanbroekmolen knoll is one of the best places to evoke the advance. Striding back to my car from the 'Pool of Peace', I realized that I was on the exact axis of the 107th Brigade. You could almost sense the pulse of over-pressure from the creeping barrage ahead and strong Ulster accent of a nearby sergeant keeping the platoon in order. It is well worth visiting Messines in high summer and rising as early as the previous night's Ypres hospitality will allow; all morning I was treated to clear blue skies and the thick haze that so many contemporary accounts refer to.

Up onto the ridge, the villages of Messines and Wytschaete are much larger today. The New Zealand memorial lies on Messines's outskirts, parallel with the 18th Bavarian Infantry Regiment's outer ring of defences (two concrete pillboxes survive nearby). It bears the thought-provoking epitaph 'From the Uttermost Ends of the Earth'. Those Kiwis came a long way to die for Britain.

Pillboxes are also to be found on the southern end of Oosttaverne Line. As an infantryman, I was able virtually to guess where those trenches were;

the Germans sited them perfectly. Pushing further north, there is plenty of interest around Hill 60 and The Caterpillar – the railway line is in use so cuttings have been maintained. However, do not bother attempting to find White Chateau. Its foundations now lie on a golf course and I was made to feel like a trespasser (an entirely just accusation).

With so much interest, it is inevitable that museums will sprout up. One of the top attractions is the Sanctuary Wood/Hill 62 Museum with 'preserved' trenches. Though not forming part of Messines, it has illustrative potential. Unfortunately, it disappoints. The museum is little more than a jumble sale of rusting shells, irrelevant prints, stuffed animals (?!) and ubiquitous fashion mannequins in moth-eaten uniforms. The trenches sit in a confused limbo – neither left to nature nor well maintained. Definitely visit the superb Passchendaele Memorial Museum in Zonnebeke. Its focus is broad and, among other exhibits, it sports a dugout system that will conjure (though not replicate) the lives of tunnellers.

The sheer quantity of cemeteries leaves one no choice but to engage in stark reflection. Tyne Cot is infamous for its numbing scale; on Messines Ridge you will find only smaller ones in which to consider the human cost of warfare. Officially, casualties at Messines Ridge are balanced at approximately 24,500 for Second Army (8.5 per cent of total strength) and 27,400 for German Fourth Army. All figures are taken from the Official Histories. British statistics cover the period 1–12 June; half their figure is II ANZAC alone. German figures cover the period 21 May to 20 June. German figures do not include wounded who returned to duty, therefore one should add at least one-third. Also, their casualties will mostly have been sustained by Gruppe Wytschaete – a much smaller force than Plumer's attacking corps.

Either way, many thousands of young men gave their lives, often willingly, during the battle of Messines Ridge. Though light by comparison with many other Great War offensives, statistical patterns matter little to the individuals concerned. In our fascination many years later, it is all too easy to forget the manner of their fate: brutal, painful and bereft of dignity.

LEFT
Anglers enjoying the summer tranquillity of Maedelstede Farm crater. (Author's collection)

RIGHT
Preserved trenches in Sanctuary Wood are of undoubted interest but mislead by being only partially maintained: they are far too shallow and there is no fire step. (Author's collection)

FURTHER READING

Primary sources

Sources relating to Messines Ridge are best subdivided into tunnelling and the battle. Like all British Great War campaigns, original documents are held in the National Archive (Public Records Office) at Kew in London. Their collection of War Office files contains copies of all the operations orders, post-operation reports and war diaries from Second Army down to each battalion. Details of how to access this material are found on their website www.nationalarchives.gov.uk. Owing to the presence of the ANZACs, there is also a wealth of material relating to Messines at the Australian War Memorial. They have done a marvellous job of scanning files, thus sparing researchers a hefty airfare. This includes the entire official history. See www.awm.gov.au.

The Royal Engineers Museum Library in Chatham is the prime repository of private papers relating to tunnelling, as well as images. They also hold copies of tunnelling company war diaries. More information can be found at www.remuseum.org.uk. The Imperial War Museum London (www.iwm.org.uk) contains a miscellany of sources on both topics. Of particular note is their comprehensive sound archive; a gem.

German primary sources are rare. Allied bombing in World War II destroyed the Reichsarchiv in Potsdam. Some Bavarian sources survived by virtue of being held in Munich. That leaves all of the memoirs and unofficial histories written between the World Wars. Colonel Jack Sheldon has contributed hugely to English-language scholarship by translating great swathes of this material. See below.

Secondary sources

The official histories relating to Messines are as follows:

Britain

Edmonds, Brig. Gen. Sir James E., *History of the Great War – Military Operations France and Belgium 1917 – Messines and Third Ypres*, London, 1948

Australia

Bean, Charles E. W., *Official History of Australia in the War of 1914–1918*, Sydney, 1933

Germany

Anonymous, *Der Weltkrieg 1914–1918 Band II*, Berlin, 1939

The following books offer an informative examination of the battle itself:

Oldham, Peter, *Battleground Europe – Messines Ridge* Leo Cooper: London, 1999

Passingham, Ian, *Pillars of Fire – The Battle of Messines Ridge* Sutton: Stroud, 1998

For a broader perspective on Third Ypres (Passchendaele):

Macdonald, Lyn, *They called it Passchendaele* Penguin: London, 1978

Prior, Robin, and Wilson, Trevor, *Passchendaele – The Untold Story* Yale University Press: London, 1996

Sheldon, Jack, *The German Army at Passchendaele* Pen and Sword: Barnsley, 2007

For a broader perspective on mine warfare:

Barrie, Alexander, *War Underground – The Tunnellers of the Great War* Frederick Muller: London, 1961

Barton, Peter et al., *Beneath Flanders Fields* Spellmount: London, 2004

Grieve, Capt Grant W, *Tunnellers* Herbert Jenkins: London, 1936

Jones, Simon, *Underground Warfare 1914–1918* Pen & Sword: Barnsley, 2010

For a broader perspective on Plumer and the Great War:

Griffith, Paddy, *Battle Tactics of the Western Front* Yale University Press: London, 1994

Holmes, Richard, *Tommy* Harper Collins: London, 2004

Keegan, John, *The First World War* Alfred A. Knopf: London, 2000

Powell, Geoffrey, *Plumer – The Soldier's General* Leo Cooper: London, 1990

INDEX

References to illustrations are shown in **bold**.

aircraft 31, **46**, 47, 49, **50**, 51
Armin, Gen. Sixt von **17**, 17, 51, 69, 85, 90

Babington, Maj. Gen. 67
Barlow, 2nd Lt. 67
Battle Wood 66–67
Bedson, Sapper 42
BEF *see* British Expeditionary Force
Bellevue 67–69
Berlin Tunnel 39
Birdcage III 43, 92
Blauwen Molen 65
Blauwepoortbeek Valley 74, **74**, 79, 80, 82, 84, 85
blockhouses 21, 62, **62**
The Bluff 41, 59
breathing apparatus **26**, **28**, 30
Bridges, Gen. Sir Tom 10
British Expeditionary Force 7, 31–35, **32**
  1st Australian Tunnelling Company 53
  1/7th Battalion London Regiment 64
  2nd Canadian Tunnelling Company 27
  3rd Australian Division 52, 79, 83, 84, 85
  3rd New Zealand Rifle Battalion 63
  4th Australian Division 69, 71, 74, 78, 80, 83, 84
  11th Battalion, Queen's Royal West Surrey Regiment 64
  11th Division 69, 71
  12th Brigade 74, 78, 79, 82–83
  13th Brigade 79, 80
  16th Division 52, 58, 63, 66, 85, **87**
  17th Brigade 80
  19th Division 10, 63, 71
  23rd Division 67
  24th Division 69
  25th Division 63, 65
  33rd Brigade 71, 80
  36th Division 52, 63, 65, **66**, 85
  37th Australian Battalion 78, 79
  41st Division 64, 67
  44th Battalion 83
  45th Battalion 79, 83, 85
  47th Battalion 75, 83
  47th Division 64, 66, 80
  48th Battalion 83
  49th Battalion 79, 84
  49th Brigade 53, 58
  50th Battalion 85
  52nd Battalion 80, 83, 84, 85

57th Brigade 71, 80
70th Brigade 67
73rd Brigade 80
107th Brigade 92
142nd Brigade 66, 80
170th Tunnelling Company 39
171st Tunnelling Company **45**, 45
175th Tunnelling Company 39
250th Tunnelling Company 41, 42
II ANZAC Corps 17, 34–35, **79**
  battle 62, 65, 78, **81**, 83–85, **84**
  battle preparations 49, 51, **52**
  casualties 93
II Brigade Heavy Branch Machine Gun Corps 49
IX Corps 16, 33–34, 63, 66, 80, 83, 84, 85
X Corps 16, 33, 64, 66, 67, 80
Baluchi infantry 6
Canadian tunnellers 27, 40
casualties 93
Durham Light Infantry **88**
Field Artillery Brigades 47
Fifth Army 47, 91
First Army 47
Inniskilling Fusiliers 53
New Zealand Division 63, 67, 71, 83, 85
orders of battle 33–35
Queen's Battalion 66
Royal Flying Corps 31, 47, 49, 51, 67–68
Second Army 8, 33–35, 46, 47, 84, 85, 93
Surrey Rifles Battalion 66
Third Army 47
training 49
tunnelling companies 23, 38
wounded soldiers **68**
British plans 38–49
  earthquaking the ridge 38–46, **44**, **45**
  operational objectives **48**
  Plumer's preparations 46–47
bunkers *see* pillboxes

camouflets 26, **29**, 30, 40, 41, 42, 43
carbon monoxide 26, 30
The Caterpillar 39, 53, 93
Chemin des Dames 11
clay-kicking 22, 25, **28**, 30
communications difficulties 62, 71, 88
craters 55, **55**, 92
creeping barrages 31, 50, 54, **59**, 59, 63, 65, 67, 74

Damm Strasse 64
Dixon, Maj. H.R. 45
Douve Valley 74, 82, 85
Dunham, Pte. Frank 64

Eden, Anthony 16
Eingreifentaktik 36, 46, 70

Factory Farm (Trench 122) **45**, 45, **62**, 67
Fagence, Pte. 64
Fanny's Farm 65
fighting tunnels 25, 26
Fingerspitzengefühl 17, 20
Fowke, Brig. Gen. George 7, 39
Franks, Maj. Gen. 50, 51
Frayling, Lt. Brian 53, 55
Frickleton, LCpl. Samuel 63
friendly fire 83
Füsslein, Oberstleutnant Otto von 38, 90

Gallwey, Pte. Wilfred 75
gas 51–52
Gegenangriff 70
Gegenstoss 36, 69–70
geology 21, **28–29**, 30, **40**, 41, 42, 43
geophones **24**, 25
German Army 19–21, 35
  1st Field Artillery Regiment 82
  1st Guards Reserve Division 69, 70, 82
  1st Guards Reserve Regiment 79
  2nd Battalion, 4th Grenadier Regiment 51
  2nd Infantry Division 37, 70
  3rd (Bavarian) Infantry Division 51, 69, 70
  4th (Bavarian) Infantry Division 37
  5th Bavarian Infantry Regiment 82
  5th Bavarian Reserve Regiment 70
  7th Infantry Division 69, 70, 71, 83
  11th Infantry Division 83
  17th Bavarian Infantry Regiment 62, 63
  18th Bavarian Infantry Regiment 63, 78, 92
  33rd Fusilier Regiment 55
  35th Infantry Division 37, 69, 70
  40th Infantry Division 37, 51, 70
  165th Infantry Regiment 83
  204th Infantry Division 37, 55
  413th Infantry Regiment 62
  III Battalion, 17th Bavarian Infantry Regiment 62
  orders of battle 35
  Eingreif divisions **36**, **71**, 90, 91
  Gruppe system 17, 70
  Gruppe Wytschaete 37, 51, 59, 64, 70, 83, 85
  Pioniere **20**, 22, **22** , 23, 39, 40, 42, 43, 45

German casualties 19, 93
German plans 36–38, **37**
German prisoners **65**, 85
Gheluvelt Plain 91
Godley, Lt. Gen. Sir Alexander 17, 83, 84
Gough, Gen. Sir Hubert 11, 86–87, 91
Grand Bois 63
Grieve, Capt. Grant 23, 27
Grieve, Capt. Robert (Bob) 79
Gruppe system 17, 70

Hackett, William 26–27, **31**
Haig, Field Marshal Sir Douglas 8, 10, 11, 50, 86, 87, 90, 91
Hamilton-Gordon, Lt. Gen. Sir Alexander 16
Harington, Maj. Gen. Charles 46, 49, 52, 67
Harvey, Brig. Gen. Robert 8
Harvey, Col. Napier 23, 39
Hell's Farm 63
Hill 60: 37, 39–40, 50, 62, 93
Hill 63: **50**, 51, 92
Hill 70: **23**
Holmes, Maj. Gen. 84, 85
Hudspeth, Capt. 45
Hun's Walk 74, 82, 83, 85

Joye Farm 80

Kemmel Sand 21, 24, **28–29**, 30, 39
Kohlmüller, Maj. von 62, 63
Kruisstraat 42
Kuhl, Gen. von 37, 90

Laffert, Gen. Maximilian von 17–18
  battle 69, 70, 83, 85
  battle aftermath 90
  battle eve 51
  plans 37–38
L'Hospice 63
Lloyd George, David 11
Lumm Farm 65, 66

Maedelstede Farm 42
Menin Road **88**, 91
Messines, battle of 50–85, **89**
  II ANZAC operations **81**, 83–85
  Battle Wood 66–67
  Bellevue 67–69
  Black Line 46, 65, 66, 67, 83, 84
  bombardment 50–51
  Damm Strasse 64
  final preparations 51–53
  friendly fire 82–83
  Gegenstoss 69–70
  Messines village 62–63
  mine explosions 53–55, **56–58**, 58–59

Oosttaverne Line 74–75, **75**, **76–78**, 78–79
  Plumer's Observation Line 66, 67, 71
  White Chateau 64
  Wytschaete village 66
  Zero Hour 52–53, 55, 58
Messines Ridge 6–7, 83, 84, 86, 92
  geology 21, **28–29**, 30, 41–42, 43
  model 49, **49**
Messines village 62–63, 92
mine craters 55, **55**, 92
mining operations 7, 21–27, **24**, **28–29**, 30, 38–46, **40**, **41**
  breathing apparatus 26, **28**, 30
  clay-kicking 22, 25, **28**, 30
  'Great Shield' machine 40–41
  mine blast **10**, 53, **54**
  schematic **44**
  shaftheads **23**, 24
  structural collapse 25–26
Montgomery, Field Marshal 88
Morland, Lt. Gen. Sir Thomas 16
mules, use of **69**
museums 93

Neuve Chapelle 25–26
Norton-Griffiths, Sir John 7–8, 22, **22**, 38, 39

Ontario Farm 43, 59
Oosttaverne Line 92
  British plans 46
  capture of 70, 74–75, **75**, **76–77**, 78–79, 80
  friendly fire 83
  German plans 37
Oosttaverne Wood 66, 67
Operation *Alberich* 19
Oxygen Trench 74

Passchendaele 90–91
Peckham Farm 42, 55
Pétain, Général 11
Petit Bois 40–42, 53, **56–57**, 58
Petit Douve farm 43
phosgene gas 51–52
Pilckem Ridge 8, 91
pillboxes 21, **21**, 51, 74–75, **75**, **76–77**, 78, 79, 92
Ploegsteert Wood 43, 51, 52
Plumer, Gen. Sir Herbert 8, 11, 16, **16**
  battle 67, 68–69, 74, 83, 85, 88
  battle aftermath 86, 87, 91
  battle eve 52
  preparations 46–47, 50
  relationship with Haig 10
  troops' training 49
Poelcappelle 91
Polygon Wood 91

Quetschungen 38

Rawlinson, Gen. Sir Henry 8, 11
RFC *see* British Expeditionary Force: Royal Flying Corps
Rupprecht, Kronprinz 37, 85, 90
Russell, Maj. Gen. Andrew 63

Schaefer, Karl 51
Schumacher, Paul 55
siege warfare 87
Siegfried Stellung 11, 19
Sixt von Armin, Gen. *see* Armin, Gen. Sixt von
Spanbroekmolen 37, 42, 53, 55, 92
Spoil Bank 66, 67, 80, 85
St Eloi **20**, 40

tanks 31–32, 74
  Mk. IV 49, 63, **65**, 65
Third Ypres **88**, **89**, 90–91
Thomas, Hauptmann 63
Thümmelschloss 62, 63
tunnellers 23, 26–27, 38, 45
'tunneller's friends' 26, **26**
tunnels *see* mining operations

Van Hove Farm 80
Vimy Ridge 25, 47

Wambeek Valley 80
Warneton Line 38, 70, 83, 85
weapons
  British Expeditionary Force 32, 47, 86
    18-pdr guns **32**, 53–54
    artillery 70, 88
    bayonets **79**
    howitzers **43**, 51
    Lee-Enfield rifles 82
    Lewis light machine guns 32, 74, 82
    Mills Bombs 32
    rifle bombs 32
    Stokes trench mortars 64
  German 47, 82
    7.7cm field guns **82**
    21cm heavy mortars **37**
    machine guns 20
    Maxim 08/15 guns 20, **76**, 78
Wenninger, Gen. von 70
Westacott, Lt. John 27
White Chateau 41, 64, 66, 67, 93
Williams, Thomas 26–27
Woodward, Capt. Oliver 53
Wytschaete **6**, **62**, **66**, 66, 92
Wytschaete Wood 63

Ypres 5, 8, 92
Ypres Salient 5–6, **9**
Yukon packs 68